DOCUMENTS OF OUR ANCESTORS

A Selection
of Reproducible Genealogy Forms
and Tips for Using Them

by Michael J. Meshenberg

Avotaynu
Teaneck, NJ 07666
1996

Copyright © 1996 by Michael J. Meshenberg

All rights reserved. Purchaser may make copies of the forms in this book for personal use. Copying of the forms for any other purpose requires written permission of the publisher. No other part of this book may be reproduced or transmitted in any form or by any means, electronic or mechanical, including photocopy, recording or information retrieval system, without prior permission from the publisher. Brief passages may be quoted with proper attribution.

Requests for permission to make copies of any part of this publication should be addressed to:

> Avotaynu, Inc.
> P.O. Box 900
> Teaneck, NJ 07666

Printed in the United States of America

First Printing

Library of Congress Cataloging-in-Publication Data
Meshenberg, Michael J.
   Dcouments of your ancestors : a selection of reproducible genealogy forms and tips for using them / by Michael J. Meshenberg.
   p. cm.
   Includes bibliographical references.
   ISBN 1-886223-01-7 (softcover)
   1. Genealogy—Forms. I. Title
CS24.M47 1996   929'.1—dc20   96-24596
                                                                                                         CIP

CONTENTS

INTRODUCTION vii
   How to Use this Book viii
   General Tips on Archival Research and Recording viii
   Abbreviations Used ix
   Some Qualifiers x

PART I. U.S. GOVERNMENT RECORDS 1
   U.S. Census Records 2
      Soundex Family Card 5
      Soundex Individual Card 6
      Census Form BC-600: Application for Search of Census Records 7
   Passenger Arrival Records 11
      New York Passenger Lists Index Cards 14
      Order for Copies of Ship Passenger Arrival Records 17
      Passenger Arrival Abstract 19
      Customs List of Passengers: 1 January 1883 – 16 June 1897 21
      Manifest of Alien Passengers : 16 June 1897 – 5 September 1903 23
      Manifest of Alien Passengers: 5 September 1903 – 30 June 1907 25
      Manifest of Alien Passengers: 1 July 1907 – 4 December 1913 27
      List or Manifest of Alien Passengers: 5 December 1913 – 31 August 1917 30
      List or Manifest of Alien Passengers: 1 September 1917 – After 31 December 1920 33
   World War I Draft Registrations 37
      National Archives—Southeast Region: World War I Registration Card Request 39
      WWI Draft Registration Card 41
   Naturalization Records and Alien Registration Records 43
      U.S. Department of Justice: Form G-639—Freedom of Information/Privacy Act Request 46
      Naturalization Abstract 48
      Declaration of Intention, Form 2202: September 27, 1906 – July 1, 1929 51
      Declaration of Intention, Form 2202 L-A: July 1, 1929 – January 13, 1941 52
      Declaration of Intention, Form N-315: January 13, 1941 – (voluntary after December 24, 1952) . 53
      Old Law (pre-1906) Petition for Naturalization 54
      Petition for Naturalization, Form 2204: 1913 – June 30, 1929 55
      Petition for Naturalization, Form 2204 L-A: July 1, 1929 – January 13, 1941 57
      Petition for Naturalization, Form N-405: January 1, 1941 – 58
      Immigration and Naturalization Service, Alien Registration Form 59
   Veterans Records 61
      National Archives Order for Copies of Veterans Record 62
   Social Security Records 65
      Social Security Death Index: Individual Record 67
      Application for Account Number, Form SS-5 68

PART II. NEW YORK STATE RECORDS 69
   New York State Census 70
      New York State Census Recording Form 72
   New York State Vital Records 73
      General Information and Application for Genealogical Services 74
      New York State Department of Health: A Verified Transcript from the Register of Live Births . . . 76
      New York State Department of Health: Marriage License 77
      New York State Department of Health: Certificate of Death 78

PART III. NEW YORK CITY RECORDS 79
   New York City Vital Records 80
      The City of New York — Department of Health: Application for a Birth Record 84
      The City of New York — Department of Health: Application for a copy of a Death Record . . 86
      New York City, Department of Records and Information Services, Municipal Archives:
         Genealogy Collections 87
      New York City, Department of Records and Information Services, Municipal Archives
         Application for a Search and/or Certified Copy of a Birth Record 88
      New York City, Department of Records and Information Services, Municipal Archives
         Application for a Search and/or Certified Copy of a Marriage Record 89
      New York City, Department of Records and Information Services, Municipal Archives
         Application for a Search and/or Certified Copy of a Death Record 90
      City of New York: Certificate and Record of Birth 91
      City of New York: Certificate and Record of Marriage 92
      Department of Health of the City of New York, Bureau of Records Standard
         Certificate of Death: ca. 1928 93
      Department of Health of the City of New York, Bureau of Records Standard
         Certificate of Death: ca. 1936 94
      Department of Health of the City of New York, Bureau of Records Standard
         Certificate of Death: ca. 1946 95
      Department of Health of the City of New York, Bureau of Records Standard
         Certificate of Death: ca. 1989 97
      The City of New York — Office of the City Clerk, Marriage License Bureau,
         In-Person Request for Marriage Record Search & Transcript 98
   New York City Voter Registration Form 99
      Board of Elections of the City of New York, Brooklyn Borough Office
         Application for Voting Information 101
      New York City Board of Elections Voter Registration Ledger Book 102

PART IV: INTERNATIONAL AND OTHER RECORDS 103
   International Tracing Service (ITS) 104
      American Red Cross Tracing Inquiry: Form 1609 106
      International Tracing Service: Index Card of Victim Information 108
      International Tracing Service: Tracking Record 109
      International Tracing Service: Index Record 110
      International Tracing Service: Index Card of an Inquiry 111
   Hamburg Emigration Lists 112
      Hamburg Emigration Office Search Form 114
      Hamburg Passenger Record: Regular Index Record 116
      Hamburg Passenger Record 117
   Polish Vital Records 118
      Polish Birth Record (Post-1826) 120
      Polish Marriage Record (Post-1826) 121
      Polish Death Record (Post-1826) 122
   American Gathering of Jewish Holocaust Survivors 123
      National Registry of Jewish Holocaust Survivors, Registration Form 124
      National Register of Jewish Holocaust Survivors, Search Form 126
   The Church of Jesus Christ of Latter-day Saints: Request for Photocopies 127
      The Church of Jesus Christ of Latter-day Saints: Request for Photocopies 128
   Yad Vashem Pages of Testimony 130
      Yad Vashem: A Page of Testimony 132

Hebrew Immigrant Aid Society (HIAS) Location Service 133
Hebrew Immigrant Aid Society (HIAS) Location Service Search Form 134
Jewish Agency: Search Bureau for Missing Relatives 136
Jewish Agency: Search Bureau for Missing Relatives Search Request Form 137

About the Author 138

INTRODUCTION

Genealogists rely on official documents for most of their ancestral information. Copies of vital records, naturalizations, census enumerations, passenger arrivals, and other less common sources represent key events in the lives of ancestors that must be recorded accurately. Most of the time, photocopies can be made from a microfilm, microfiche, book, or other source. Often, however, the quality of the document is poor and the copy made may not be fully legible, or it may literally be impossible to reproduce. Every genealogist has had the painstaking experience of trying to make out an obscure name or date off a microfilm reader.

Having good recording forms helps assure the accurate copying of this essential information.

Much of what genealogists do is tedious—looking through indexes for the elusive reference, searching a census or passenger record for a name, trying to read an old, faded document with illegible handwriting. This book is intended to try to ease some of the tedium by simplifying the recording of results.

Reproducible recording forms serve many other purposes:
- They tell the researcher the exact information to expect before conducting a search, and, therefore, to decide whether to purchase the record.
- They provide a checklist to assure that all the information on a document is recorded.
- They provide a uniform and consistent format that avoids random notes on scraps of paper.
- When used in a repository, they enable information to be copied from the original source.
- They provide an alternate means to share information among family members or to compare information among documents.
- The researcher may want the information on the original record, but not want to pay for a certified copy.

This publication helps fill a void in the material available to genealogists by providing an extensive set of recording and search forms in a format that allows easy reproduction. While many forms are provided, the selection is not comprehensive. The selection includes a large number of forms used to record and obtain data from federal sources, New York State and New York City, plus a variety of other organizations that have material of value to genealogists.

This book offers only some general guidance on finding and using these materials. It assumes the reader has at least a working knowledge of sources and finding aids. It doesn't substitute for the in-depth knowledge required before conducting research in an unfamiliar set of records. It also doesn't duplicate research information available elsewhere but suggests some useful reference sources that can explain how to search these materials most efficiently and effectively. Finally, included in each section are some user tips to make the search and recording easier and quicker, things that the author has discovered by trial and lots of error (and wasted time).

Although the forms here should be valuable for many genealogists, the set should be particularly beneficial for Jewish genealogists, many of whose ancestors lived for a time in New York City or New York State. In a sense, this is a personal choice; I initiated this collection to serve my own research needs and have come to recognize that there are many others who have the same needs.

Three types of forms are provided here; Reproduction, Replica, Abstract.

- Reproduction: Photocopy of a blank original.
- Replica: Computer-generated, in a format approximating the originals. Originals generally were

not available. Further, these documents typically were maintained in the same or similar formats for many years. In two instances—New York Passenger Arrival Manifests and New York City Death Records—replicas of sample years are provided.
- Abstract: Because some forms often changed, sometimes significantly, an abstract is provided to record all the information likely to be found in a range of years. The originals may include lots of standardized text or instructions that is not necessary to be reproduced on abstracts.

Not included here are standard genealogy recording forms such as family group sheets, descendant charts, or ancestral charts. These are widely available and there is no point in reproducing them here. And, with the increasing use of computers to maintain family records, the use of hand-entered charts is diminishing. A good source of reproducible forms is: William Dollarhide, *Managing a Genealogical Project*. It is available from Ancestry, Inc., P.O. Box 476, Salt Lake City, UT 84110. Also of value is: Thomas Jay Kemp, *International Vital Records Handbook,* which contains copies of applications for vital records for all states and many foreign countries. It can be purchased from the publisher, Genealogical Publishing Co., 1001 N. Calvert Street, Baltimore, MD 21202. Both also are available from Avotaynu, Inc., P.O. Box 900, Teaneck, NJ 07666. Some forms also are available on the Internet; see JewishGen Infofile, "Genealogy Forms," <http://www.jewishgen.org>, June 1995.

How to Use this Book

Each section of this book follows the same six-part format:

- Forms Provided: Lists each of the reproducible forms included in the section.
- What Records Are Available: A general introduction to the records that can be accessed by using the forms, either in person or by contacting the issuing agency.
- Where to Find Them: Who holds the records, both the originals and copies.
- What You Need Before You Search: A guide to understanding indexes and finding aids to the records and what you must know to enable a search to be successful.
- Tips: Ideas and comments on how to use the forms, avoid pitfalls, and simplify the searching process.
- Additional Help: Bibliographic and other references to help the user more fully understand the various sets of records, what they include, and the subtleties of the search process. It should be noted here that no book of this type would now be complete without reference to the growing genealogical value of the Internet, and particularly, the World Wide Web. Although relatively little genealogical data is yet directly accessible on line, a vast amount of guidance, help, and reference material is available. The growth is explosive, and no published work can keep up to date. References are given here to what is known at the time of publication.

General Tips on Archival Research and Recording

- Similar records often change over time. The selection here does not include every possible variation in the design of each form. Rather, it tries to provide a space to record everything on all the known variations used. Specific distinctions may be noted in the discussion accompanying each form.
- Search forms (applications) and index records serve the same basic purpose: an aid to finding the actual record. As a result, the more you know about a person in the format indexed or filed, the more likely you are to find the correct record being sought—particularly if the surname is relatively common—and the more efficient will be the time spent in the repository. For example, on a copy of the index record, enter all the information you may have at home. Fill in the rest,

or correct errors, when you find the actual index record. These index records also serve as reminders of what you looked for, where, and when.
- If you are recording the information in person, check for nearby names on lists such as passenger arrivals or census records. You can learn useful things such as names of others from the same town or other relatives living at the same address even if not in the same household.
- Copy down **everything** on an index record even if you do not understand what it means. Indexing systems are highly variable and everything might be important even if you don't know why. Clerks at the repository will usually know, or you will probably figure it out. For example, copy names and information about witnesses on marriage records and informants on death records. These names can lead to discoveries of distant family members and some information about them when you start checking the records.
- Note the name of the repository, date researched, film or fiche number, and other source information of every record searched. Space is provided on most recording forms here for this information.
- A distinction sometimes is made in the information needed for mail inquiries (by application form) and in-person requests. The "What You Need . . ." sections indicate that what is needed for an in-person search generally is similar but not necessarily identical to what is required on an application. In addition to saving fees, in-person searches, where possible, have the advantage of enabling the researcher to scan indexes or groups of records for name variations, other years, etc.
- If you are visiting a Family History Center, carry a computer disk. Downloading catalog, Social Security Death Index, and other information onto your disk enables you to format the information at home in your own word processing or database software, and manipulate it for your own use. Afterward, you can maintain the results of your search as a permanent record in printed or electronic format.
- Finally, always carry a good magnifying glass.

Abbreviations Used

Certain shorthand references appear in the text:

FHL: The Family History Library of the Church of Jesus Christ of Latter Day Saints, the vast genealogy library located in Salt Lake City, Utah. A WWW homepage about the FHL is located at <ftp://ftp.cac.psu.edu/pub/genealogy/public_html/LDS.html>. Many excellent books have been written about the FHL. The JewishGen Infofile "Guide to LDS Family History Library, Salt Lake City, Utah" is accessible through the JewishGen homepage.

FHC: Family history centers, or branch libraries of the Family History Library located throughout the United States with access to the records stored in Salt Lake City.

Guzik: A reference to *Genealogical Resources in the New York Metropolitan Area,* edited by Estelle M. Guzik and published in 1989 by the Jewish Genealogical Society (New York). It lists in detail the important resources in New York and New Jersey, including New York State materials in Albany. This book is the key resource for identifying many of the specific New York City records available and how they can be accessed.

JewishGen: This refers to the Jewish Genealogy Discussion Group on the Internet, and its associated homepages on the World Wide Web (WWW). It offers lively discussions on all aspects of Jewish genealogy, publishes a growing collection of electronic resource guides called "InfoFiles," and provides numerous links to the extensive genealogical resources on the Internet. A number of JewishGen InfoFiles are cited here for additional information. Jewish Gen and all its InfoFiles can be accessed on the WWW at: <http://www.jewishgen.org/>.

NARA: The National Archives and Records Administration, the agency of the U.S. Government that maintains holdings of such major genealogical collections as censuses, passenger arrivals, naturalizations, and many others. NARA has twelve regional branches. The NARA homepage is <http://www.nara.gov>.

Some Qualifiers

The application forms reproduced here are believed to be up to date as of the time of publication. They sometimes change, so there is no guarantee they will always remain in effect. However, most changes usually are minor and experience indicates that the issuing agency will usually accept a recent form if it includes most of the needed information. Prices, of course, change more frequently, so it's usually a good idea to check first before ordering. National Center for Health Statistics, *Where to Write for Vital Records* (Washington: Superintendent of Documents, U.S. Government Printing Office, 1990) lists addresses and many phone numbers. A shortened version is available on the WWW at <gopher://gopher.gsa.gov:70/00/staff/pa/cic/misc/vital.txt>.

Forms here are intended to be reproduced for personal use and permission is granted for that purpose. Permission for reproduction in other publications must be obtained from the publisher in advance. Government forms are not copyright and can be freely reproduced for any purpose.

Part I

U.S. Government Records

U.S. Census Records

Forms Provided

    A. *Soundex Family Card (1920)*

    B. *Soundex Individual Card (1920)*

    C. *Application for Search of Census Records (Form BC-600)*

(Replicas of census recording forms are not provided here since they are available at all National Archives branches [usually for free] and at Family History Centers [at nominal cost].)

What Records Are Available

U.S. Census records are released to the public 72 years after they occur; e.g., the 1920 census was made public in April 1992. Information about what is available after 1920, how to apply, and restrictions, is contained on the reproduced form BC-600, *Application for Search of Census Records*.

Soundex (Census Index) cards are the first step in finding U.S. Census records for years 1880, 1900, and 1920. Almost all the 1890 census was lost in a fire and no soundex was prepared for 1910. Coding forms for translating names to soundex codes are available in numerous census publications, all branches of the National Archives, and at Family History Centers. Local alphabetic indexes to the 1800–60 and most of the 1870 censuses are available in genealogical libraries. (Family History Centers have a publication called *The Soundex Reference Guide* which lists the code for many names.) Many genealogy computer programs can provide soundex codes automatically. Librarians or archivists can help translate the name into the soundex code. A soundex code converter is available on the WWW at <http://www.rand.org/cgi-bin/Genea/soundex.sh>.

Where to Find Them

Microfilms of soundex cards for census data are available wherever Census records are located. Principal sources are:
1. Branches of the National Archives and Records Administration.
2. Family History Centers (films must be ordered).
3. Many local and genealogical libraries have soundex and census films for the area or region.

What You Need Before You Search

1. Name of the head of household (cards are in soundex order by heads of household; others in the household are not indexed).
2. Preferably:
   - Age of head of household.
   - County of residence. Some idea of the residence address is helpful, particularly if the name is common.
   - Names and estimated ages of others in the household.

Tips

- There are two types of soundex cards: (1) Family and (2) Individual (person living alone, boarding in an institution, or residing in another household). The cards used in 1920 and 1900 are virtually identical.

- Before you arrive at the repository, make copies of the index cards and pencil in all the information you can about people you are searching for, e.g., names, ages, addresses, etc., so you can readily identify the actual card when you find it.

- When you find the card, copy down EVERYTHING exactly as shown, correcting your own information.

- Most important is the data in the upper right corner: Vol., E.D. (enumeration district), Sheet, Line. This provides what you need to find the exact census record.

- If the soundex card is full, check the next card; large families may have a continuation card.

- There is no soundex for the 1910 census. But many repositories, including branches of the National Archives have, on microfiche, a *1910 Census Index to City Streets and Enumeration Districts for 39 Cities.*

    The following cities are included Akron, OH; Atlanta, GA; Baltimore, MD; Canton, OH; Charlotte, NC; Chicago, IL; Cleveland, OH; Dayton, OH; Denver, CO; Detroit, MI; Washington, DC; Elizabeth, NJ; Erie, PA; Fort Wayne, IN; Kansas City, KS; Long Beach, CA; Los Angeles City and County, CA; Newark, NJ; New York City: Brooklyn, Manhattan/Bronx, Richmond (not Queens); Oklahoma City, OK; Omaha, NB; Paterson, NJ; Peoria, IL; Philadelphia, PA; Phoenix, AZ; Reading, PA; Richmond, VA; San Antonio, TX; San Diego, CA; San Francisco, CA; Seattle, WA; South Bend, IN; Tampa, FL; Tulsa, OK; Wichita, KS; Youngstown, OH.

- These indexes provide the enumeration district for each street address and, if the address is known, are as simple to use as the soundex cards.

- It is very helpful to bring a good map of the county or city in which you are searching, one showing all streets. For New York City boroughs, for example, Hagstrom maps show street addresses every few blocks. Recent CD-ROM versions of atlases, such as DeLorme's, *Street Atlas U.S.A.*, provide current addresses for the entire country. These can be very useful in cities that have remained relatively unchanged (but not in suburbs).

- Many Family History Centers have folders showing step-by-step methods for searching for information in each census starting with 1890.

Additional Help

Guzik, *Genealogical Resources in the New York Metropolitan Area,* provides information on all locations in the New York area that hold census records.

Hamilton, Ann B., *A Researcher's Guide to United States Census Availability 1790–1920* (Bowie, MD: Heritage Books, Second Edition, 1987).

JewishGen InfoFile, "Soundex Coding," <http://www.jewishgen.org>, Feb. 1996.

National Archives Trust Fund Board,
    _____, *Federal Population Censuses, 1790–1890: A Catalog of Microfilm Copies of the Schedules,* 1979.

    _____, *1900 Federal Population Census: A Catalog of Microfilm Copies of the Schedules,* 1978.

    _____, *The 1910 Federal Population Census: A Catalog of Microfilm Copies of the Schedules,* 1982.

    _____, *The 1920 Federal Population Census: Catalog of National Archives Microfilms,* 2nd edition, 1992.

_____, *Guide to Genealogical Research in the National Archives,* Revised 1985.
(All these are available on the World Wide Web at <http://www.nara.gov>).

U.S. Bureau of the Census, *Availability of Census Records about Individuals,* Publication No. CFF No. 2 (rev.). (Includes a list of items covered in every census, 1790-1990.)

Soundex Family Card

_____ VOL. _____ E.D. _____
(HEAD OF FAMILY)
                            SHEET _____ LINE _____

_____ _____ _____ _____
(COLOR) (AGE)   (BIRTHPLACE)   (CITIZENSHIP)

_____
    (COUNTY)

_____ _____ _____
    (CITY)   (STREET)   (HOUSE NO.)

OTHER MEMBERS OF FAMILY

NAME	RELATIONSHIP	AGE	BIRTHPLACE	CITIZENSHIP

Repository _____; Film number _____; Volume and page_____;
Date researched _____; Copy of original made _____?; Researcher's Notes:

Soundex Individual Card

_____ VOL. _____ E.D. _____
(INDIVIDUAL)
                                                                                          SHEET _____ LINE _____

_____ _____ _____ _____
(COLOR)   (AGE)   (BIRTHPLACE)   (CITIZENSHIP)

_____
(COUNTY)

_____ _____ _____
(CITY)   (STREET)   (HOUSE NO.)

ENUMERATED WITH _____

RELATIONSHIP TO ABOVE _____

REMARKS _____

_____

Repository _____; Film number _____; Volume and page _____;
Date researched _____; Copy of original made _____?; Researcher's Notes:

Documents of Our Ancestors

FORM BC-600
(12 93)

U.S. DEPARTMENT OF COMMERCE
BUREAU OF THE CENSUS

APPLICATION FOR SEARCH OF CENSUS RECORDS
IMPORTANT INFORMATION
PLEASE READ AND FOLLOW CAREFULLY

This application is for use in requesting a search of census records.* Copies of these census records often are accepted as evidence of age, citizenship, and place of birth for employment, social security benefits, insurance, and other purposes.

If the applicant is located, an official transcript will be provided including the following information:

Personal Census Information	Available for census year(s)
• Census year	1910–1990
• County where taken	1910–1980
• State where taken	1910–1990
• Name	1910–1990
• Relationship to head of household	1910–1990
• Name of person in whose household you were counted	1910–1990
• Age at the time of the census	1910–1950, 1970–1990
• Date of birth	
Year and quarter	1960
Month and year	1970–1980
Year	1990
• Place of birth	1910–1950
• Citizenship if requested or if foreign born	1910–1950
• Occupation (if requested)	1910–1950

The Census Bureau's records with **INDIVIDUAL NAMES ARE NOT ON A COMPUTER.** They are on microfilm, arranged according to the address at the time of the census. Censuses are taken primarily for statistical, not legal, purposes. Attention is called to the possibility that the information shown in the census record may not agree with that given in your application. **The record must be copied exactly as it appears on the census form.** The Census Bureau CANNOT make changes even though it realizes that enumerators may have been misinformed or made mistakes in writing down the data they collected. Those agencies that accept census transcripts as evidence of age, relationship, or place of birth usually overlook minor spelling differences but would be reluctant to consider a record that was changed years later at an applicant's request.

If you authorize the Bureau of the Census to send your record to someone other than yourself, you must provide the name and address, including ZIP Code, of the other person/agency.

Birth certificates, including delayed birth certificates, are **not issued** by the Bureau of the Census. You can obtain the birth certificate from the Health Department or the Department of Vital Statistics of the state in which the applicant was born.

The average time it should take you to fill out the BC-600, "Application for Search of Census Records", including the time spent reading instructions is 12 minutes.

If you have any questions regarding these estimates or any other aspect of this form, please call or write the Associate Director for Administration, Paperwork Reduction Project 0607-0117, Room 2027, Bureau of the Census, Washington, D.C. 20233 and to the Office of Management and Budget, Paperwork Reduction Project 0607-0117, Washington, D.C. 20503.

---

* Information from 1920 and earlier censuses is public information and is available from the National Archives.

The completed application should be mailed to the Bureau of the Census, P.O. Box 1545, Jeffersonville, IN 47131, together with a money order or check payable to "Commerce–Census."

INSTRUCTIONS FOR COMPLETING THIS FORM
PRINT OR TYPE INFORMATION EXCEPT SIGNATURE
PLEASE FOLLOW NUMBERED INSTRUCTIONS

1. **Purpose**

    The purpose for which the information is desired must be shown so that a determination may be made under 13 U.S.C. 8(a) that the record is required for proper use. For proof of age, most agencies require documents closest to date of birth; therefore we suggest you complete information for the EARLIEST CENSUS AFTER DATE OF BIRTH.

2. **Signature**

    Each application requires a signature. The signature should be the same as that shown on the line captioned "full name of person whose census record is requested." When the application is for a census record concerning another person, the requester must sign the application, and the authority of the requester must be furnished as stated in instruction 3 below. If signed by marking (X), please indicate the name of the person whose mark it is and have witnesses sign as instructed. IF SIGNATURE IS PRINTED, please indicate that is the usual signature.

3. **Confidential information given to other than person to whom it relates**

    (a) Census information is confidential and ordinarily will not be furnished to another person unless the person to whom it relates authorizes this in the space provided or if there is other proper authorization as indicated in 3(b), 3(c), and 3(d).

    (b) Minor children – Information regarding a child who has at this time not reached the legal age of 18 may be obtained upon the written request of either parent or guardian.

    (c) Mentally incompetent persons – Information regarding persons who are mentally incompetent may be obtained upon the written request of the legal representative, supported by a certified copy of the court order naming such legal representative.

    (d) **Deceased persons – If the record requested relates to a deceased person, the application MUST be signed by (1) a blood relative in the immediate family (parent, brother, sister, or child), (2) the surviving wife or husband, (3) the administrator or executor of the estate, or (4) a beneficiary by will, or insurance. IN ALL CASES INVOLVING DECEASED PERSONS, a certified copy of the death certificate MUST be furnished, and the relationship to the deceased MUST be stated on the application. Legal representatives MUST also furnish a certified copy of the court order naming such legal representatives; and beneficiaries MUST furnish legal evidence of such beneficiary interest.**

4. **Fee required**

    The $40.00 fee is for a search of one census for one person only. The time required to complete a search depends upon the number of cases on hand at the particular time and the difficulty encountered in searching a particular case. The normal processing time requires 4 to 6 weeks. Since the fee covers return postage, do not send a stamped self-addressed envelope with the application.

    No more than one census will be searched and the results furnished for one fee. Should it be necessary to search more than one census to find the record, you will be notified to send another fee before another search is made. Tax monies are not available to furnish the information. **If a search has been made, the fee cannot be returned even if the information is not found.**

5. **Full schedules (For Genealogy)**

    The full schedule is the complete one-line entry of personal data recorded for that individual ONLY. The names of other persons will not be listed. If the applicant specifies "full schedule," the Census Bureau will furnish, in addition to the regular transcript, whatever other information appears on the named person's record in the original schedule, but only for THAT PERSON. In this case the information is typed on a facsimile of the original census schedule and verified as a true copy. There is an additional charge of $10.00 for EACH full schedule requested.

    The Census Bureau also will provide "full schedule" information for those other members of the same household for whom authorizations are furnished. (See Instruction 3 for authorization requirements). A fee of $10.00 is required for each person listed on the full schedule.

    LIMITATIONS — Certain information, such as place of birth, citizenship, and occupation, is available only for census years 1910 through 1950. Full schedule information is not available for census years 1970, 1980, and 1990.

6. **Census years 1910–1920–1930–1940– 1950– 1960–1970–1980–1990**

    The potential of finding an individual's census record is increased when the respondent provides thorough and accurate address information FOR THE DAY THESE CENSUSES WERE TAKEN. If residing in a city AT THE TIME THESE CENSUSES WERE TAKEN, it is necessary to furnish the house number, the name of the street, city, county, state, and the name of the parent or other head of household with whom residing at the time of the census. If residing in a rural area, it is VERY IMPORTANT to furnish the township, district, precinct or beat, AND the direction and number of miles from the nearest town.

    1990 Request — It is VERY IMPORTANT to provide a house number and street name or rural route and box number. Always include a ZIP Code.

7. **Locator Map (optional)**

    Box 7 is provided for a sketch of the area where the applicant lived at the time of the requested census.

IF YOU NEED HELP FILLING OUT THIS APPLICATION, PLEASE CALL 812-285-5314, MONDAY THROUGH FRIDAY 7:00 A.M. THROUGH 4:30 P.M. EASTERN TIME

FORM BC-600
(12-93)

U.S. DEPARTMENT OF COMMERCE
BUREAU OF THE CENSUS

OMB No. 0607-0117 Approval expires 01-31-96

APPLICATION FOR SEARCH OF CENSUS RECORDS

RETURN TO: Bureau of the Census, P.O. Box 1545, Jeffersonville, IN 47131

DO NOT USE THIS SPACE – OFFICIAL USE ONLY	
$ _____ (Fee) ☐ Money Order ☐ Check ☐ Other	Case number
Papers received (itemize)	Returned
Received by	Date
Returned by	Date

NAME OF APPLICANT

1. Purpose for which record is to be used (See Instruction 1)
- ☐ Passport (date required) _____
- ☐ Proof of age
- ☐ Genealogy
- ☐ Other – Please specify

I certify that information furnished about anyone other than the applicant will not be used to the detriment of such person or persons by me or by anyone else with my permission.

2. Signature – Do not print (Read instruction 2 carefully before signing)

PRESENT MAILING ADDRESS
- Number and street
- City / State / ZIP Code
- Telephone number (Include area code)

3. If the census information is **to be sent to someone other than the person whose record is requested**, give the name and address, including ZIP Code, of the other person or agency.

This authorizes the Bureau of the Census to send the record to: (See instruction 3)

Signature
IF SIGNED BY MARK (X), TWO WITNESSES MUST SIGN HERE
Signature

NOTICE – Intentionally falsifying this application may result in a fine of $10,000 or 5 years of imprisonment, or both (title 18, U.S. Code, section 1001).

4. FEE REQUIRED: (See instructions 4 and 5) A check or money order (**DO NOT SEND CASH**) payable to "Commerce – Census" must be sent with the application. This fee covers the cost of a search of no more than one census year for one person only.

5. Fee required .... $ 40.00
- _____ extra copies @ $2.00 $ _____
- _____ full schedules @ $10.00 $ _____
   (for genealogy)
- **TOTAL amount enclosed** $ _____

FULL NAME OF PERSON WHOSE CENSUS RECORD IS REQUESTED

First name	Middle name	Maiden name (If any)	Present last name	Nicknames

Date of birth (If unknown, estimate)	Place of birth (City, county, State)	Race	Sex	Nicknames

Full name of father (Stepfather, guardian, etc.)

Full maiden name of mother (Stepmother, e.c.)

First marriage (Name of husband or wife)	Year married (Approximate)	Second marriage (Name of husband or wife)	Year married (Approximate)

Names of brothers and sisters

Name and relationship of all other persons living in household (Aunts, uncles, grandparents, lodgers, etc.)

PLEASE COMPLETE REVERSE SIDE

GIVE PLACE OF RESIDENCE FOR APPROPRIATE CENSUS DATE *(SEE INSTRUCTIONS 1 AND 6)*

Census date	Number and street *(Read instruction 6 first)*	City, town, township *(Read instruction 6 first)*	County and State	Name of person with whom living *(Head of household)*	Relationship of head of household
April 15, 1910 *(See instruction 6)*					
Jan. 1, 1920 *(See instruction 6)*					
April 1, 1930 *(See instruction 6)*					
April 1, 1940 *(See instruction 6)*					
April 1, 1950 *(See instruction 6)*					
April 1, 1960 *(See instruction 6)*					
April 1, 1970 *(See instruction 6)*					
April 1, 1980 *(See instruction 6)*					
April 1, 1990 *(See instruction 6)*	ZIP Code				

7. LOCATOR MAP *(Optional)* PLEASE DRAW A MAP OF WHERE THE APPLICANT LIVED, SHOWING ANY PHYSICAL FEATURES, LANDMARKS, INTERSECTING ROADS, CLOSEST TOWNS, ETC., THAT MAY AID IN LOCATING THE APPLICANT FOR THE CENSUS YEAR REQUESTED.

FORM BC-600 (1-21-93)

HAVE YOU SIGNED THE APPLICATION AND ENCLOSED THE CORRECT FEES?

Passenger Arrival Records

Forms Provided

A. *New York Passenger List Index Card: 16 June 1897 – 16 July 1902*
B. *New York Passenger List Index Card: July 1902 – May 1905*
C. *New York Passenger List Index Card: May 1904 – July 1906*
D. *New York Passenger List Index Card: March 1905 – July 1906*
E. *New York Passenger List Index Card: September 1906 – September 1907*
F. *New York Passenger List Index Card: October 1906 – January 1907*
G. *New York Passenger List Index Card: June 1907 – May 1908*
H. *New York Passenger List Index Card: December 1903 – June 1910*
I. *New York Passenger List Index Card: July 1910 – 1937*
J. *New York Passenger List Index Card: 1937 – June 1942*
K. *New York Passenger List Index Card: July 1942 – December 1943*
L. *Order for Copies of Ship Passenger Arrival Records* (NATF Form 81)
(Note: This is a multi-part form and cannot be reproduced. An original must be requested from General Reference Branch (NNRG) National Archives and Records Administration, 7th and Pennsylvania Avenue, N.W., Washington, DC 20408, or from regional branches.)
M. *Passenger Arrival Abstract*
N. *Customs List of Passengers: 1 January 1883 – 16 June 1897*
O. *Manifest of Alien Passengers: 16 June 1897 – 5 September 1903*
P. *Manifest of Alien Passengers: 5 September 1903 – 30 June 1907*
Q. *Manifest of Alien Passengers: 1 July 1907 – 4 December 1913*
R. *List or Manifest of Alien Passengers: 5 December 1913 – 31 August 1917*
S. *List or Manifest of Alien Passengers: 1 September 1917 – After 31 December 1920*

What Records Are Available

Ship passenger arrival lists are available for most American ports from the National Archives and Records Administration—in some cases from the very earliest years of immigration virtually up to the present day. The various regional branches have selected sets of these lists. Many, but not all, are indexed. Form 81 summarizes the records available. A complete list of NARA holdings is included in *Guide to Genealogical Research in the National Archives* (see below). These records are extraordinarily valuable sources of information about immigrants, and a great deal has been written about them. Colletta's book, *They Came in Ships,* is among the most useful practical guides. Other good sources of information about what these lists contain and how to use them are listed below.

Where to Find Them

The National Archives headquarters in Washington, DC, contains microfilms of the original lists and can be searched by mail using Form 81. Holdings of its branches vary. The Family History Library is believed to have a complete duplicate set. Selected sets also are found in many local and genealogical libraries.

What You Need Before You Search

If you are searching for an immigrant's passenger arrival record in an index, you will need to know:
– Port of arrival.
– Original name (usually the one used before arrival since lists were prepared prior to departure or on board ship).
– Approximate age at arrival.
– Approximate date of arrival.
   It is useful to know this information even if searching a ship's manifest without using an index, to

distinguish one passenger from another.

Not all lists are indexed; for example, no indexes exist for the Port of New York for the years 1847–96 nor for 1949–present (see the request form for details on holdings). But the Glazier reference, below, offers an alternative method of searching. The LDS church, as well, has begun a massive effort to computerize Ellis Island records, but no publication date has been announced.

Tips

Passenger Arrival <u>Abstract</u>:
- Reproductions of index cards and facsimiles of passenger lists are provided here. An abstract form also is provided as an alternative. The abstract contains spaces for all information included on indices and manifests used from at least 1897 on. Particularly when the arrival year is not known before visiting the archive, it may be simpler to reproduce a few copies of the abstract, copy down all the information found, and transfer the results later to the appropriate form as a permanent record.

Passenger Arrival <u>Indexes</u>:
- How to read the index cards:
  1897–1902: Filed alphabetically by surname, then by given name.
  1902–43: Surnames A-C filed by soundex code, then alphabetically by the first letter or first two letters of the given name, then by date of ship arrival (or volume number when date is not given). Surnames D-Z are filed by soundex code, then alphabetically by given name, then those with no age given (years 1903–10), then by age at arrival.
  What the fields mean: Code = soundex code; Name = full name of passenger; Steamer = name of vessel; Line = steamship company; Date = arrival date at port of New York; Group = page number of manifest. (Where the page numbers are found—1897–1902: usually in top right corner; 1902–08: usually in pencil or stamped at top left; 1908–43: usually numbers are stamped at bottom left); List = the line number on the manifest page (up to 30 lines per page).
  Special symbols: Asterisk(*) = 1–4 asterisks in upper right corner signifies that additional cross-reference cards were made for hyphenated surnames; surnames De, Di, Van,, or Von; and Catholic sisters; CR# = sometimes used in place of group, list, and volume numbers and refer to the passenger's naturalization number. The name of the vessel and date of arrival can be requested from: INS, 26 Federal Plaza, New York, NY 10278.
- Facsimiles of eleven index cards are provided for five periods from 1897 to 1943; these can be used to selectively search through indexes. There is some overlap in the dates the various cards were in use.
- Cards often are misfiled; also check for alternate name spellings.
- For unindexed ports or years, other sources such as naturalization records must be used to determine the name of the ship and date of arrival. The National Archives' *Immigrant and Passenger Arrivals* has a detailed description of the microfilmed indexes available. Colletta offers good advice on using them.
- Prepare a stack of the index cards facsimiles when you're looking for several different people. Before you leave home, pencil this information on the index cards to aid in the search.
- As shown on the index card facsimiles, information on indexes varies widely. The index record for New York shows the volume number (literally the books in which the lists are bound). This can be translated into the year by checking the Family History Library catalog record under the following headings: 1. United States - Emigration and immigration; 2. New York, New York (City) - Emigration and immigration; I. National Archives microfilm publications, T0621; II. National Archives microfilm publications, T0715; and, III. National Archives microfilm publications, T0519.
- The microfilmed copies are tiny and sometimes frustratingly hard to read because of poor quality microfilming. Carry a magnifying glass.
- Children traveling with their families generally are not indexed; you will need to know the name of the head of the traveling party (father, mother, older sibling, etc.)

Passenger Arrival <u>Lists</u>:
- Information requested from passengers varied over time, e.g. very little information was collected prior to

1819 and, even after 1897, some modifications were made in the column headings on the manifest. The recording forms provided here are believed to represent all the information included within each period and will let the researcher know exactly what to expect before searching.
- As a result, the order of the information on the abstract may not strictly follow the column headings.
- Check the manifest to see who else was traveling with this person, or even names of others from the same town. For example, sometimes children were escorted by a friend or relative from the same town.

Additional Help

Colletta, John P., *They Came in Ships* (Salt Lake City: Ancestry, Inc., Revised 1993).

Filby, P. William, *Passenger and Immigration Lists Bibliography, 1538–1900: Being a Guide to Published Lists of Arrivals in the United States and Canada* (Detroit: Gale Research Company, 1981; Supplement 1984; Cumulative edition, 1988).

Glazier, Ira, editor, *Migration from the Russian Empire: Lists of Passengers Arriving at the Port of New York* (Baltimore, MD: Genealogical Publishing Company, 1995) [vol. I: January 1875 – September 1882; vol. II: October 1882 – April 1886].

"Immigration and Naturalization," pp. 1–6, in *The Encyclopedia of Jewish Genealogy, Volume I: Sources in the United States and Canada,* edited by Arthur Kurzweil and Miriam Weiner, 1991 (Northvale, NJ: Jason Aronson, Inc., 1991).

JewishGen InfoFile, "How to Interpret Index to Passenger Arrivals List #T-621 (Soundex)," <http://www.jewishgen.org>, Sept. 1995.

JewishGen InfoFile, "JewishGen FAQ - Frequently Asked Questions," Part 10, Passenger Lists, <http://www.jewishgen.org>, April 1996 (updated monthly).

National Archives Trust Fund Board, *National Archives Microfilm Publications.* Second Edition. (Atlanta, GA: The Board, 1991).

_____, *Guide to Genealogical Research in the National Archives*, (Washington, DC: U.S. National Archives and Record Administration, Revised 1985).

National Archives and Records Administration, *Immigrant and Passenger Arrivals: A Select List of National Archives Microfilm Publications,* 1983.

Serene, Frank H., "Sources at the National Archives for Genealogical and Local History Research: American Immigrant Genealogy, Ship Passenger Lists," in *Prologue, Journal of the National Archives,* vol. 17, no. 2 (Summer 1985), pages 112-121.

Tepper, Michael, *American Passenger Arrival Records: A Guide to the Records of Immigrants at American Ports by Sail and Steam* (Baltimore: Genealogical Publishing Company, Revised, 1993).

New York Passenger Lists Index Cards

Code		
Family name	Given name	Accompanied by
Place of birth (town, country, etc.)	Age Yrs/Mos — Sex M/W — S/D	Occupation — Read/Write
Race	Nationality	Last permanent residence (town, country, etc.)
Name and address of nearest relative or friend in country whence alien came		
Ever in U.S. — From — To	Where	Passage paid by
Destination and name and address of relative or friend to join there		
Money shown — Ever arrested, deported, or excluded from admission	Head tax status	
Height ft. in. — Complexion — Hair — Eyes	Distinguishing marks	
Seaport and date of landing and name of steamship		
		Group - List - Volume

Form 548-B   16 June 1897 - 16 July 1902

Repository _____ ; Film number _____ ; Volume and page _____ ; Date researched _____
Copy of original made _____ ?; Researcher's Notes:

New York Passenger Lists Index Cards

Code _____
Name: _____ Age: _____
and _____ members of family.
Citizen of: _____
Steamer: _____ Line: _____
Date: _____ New York.
Group No.: _____ List No.: _____

Form 1502A July 1902 - May 1905

Code: _____
Name: _____ Age: _____
and _____ members of family.
Citizen of: _____
Steamer: _____ Line: _____
Date: _____ New York.
Group No. _____ List No.: _____

N.Y. Form 27 May 1904 - July 1906

Code: _____
Name: _____
and _____ members of family.   AGE: _____
Steamer: _____   Sex: _____
Date: _____ New York.
Group No. _____ List No.: _____

Typed card March 1905 - July 1906

Code: _____
Name: _____ Age: _____
Sex: _____ Citizen of: _____
Steamer: _____ Line: _____
Date: _____ New York.
Group No. _____ List No.: _____

N.Y. Form 27 September 1906 - September 1907

Repository _____; Film number _____; Volume and page _____; Date researched _____
Copy of original made _____?; Researcher's Notes:

A Selection of Reproducible Genealogy Forms and Tips for Using Them

New York Passenger Lists Index Cards

N.Y. Form 27
October 1906 - January 1907

Code: _____
Name: _____ Age: _____
Group No.: _____ List No.: _____ Sex: _____
Citizen of: _____
Steamer: _____ Line: _____
Date: _____ New York.

N.Y. Form 27 June 1907 - May 1908

Name: _____ Age: _____
Group No.: _____ List No.: _____ Sex: _____
Citizen of: _____
S.S. _____ Line: _____
Date: _____ New York.

December 1903 - June 1910

Code
Name — Group List Vessel Date

July 1910 - 1937

Code
Name — Age/Sex List Group Volume

1937 - June 1942

Code — Month/year
Name — Age/Sex List Group Volume
Vessel

July 1942 - December 1943

Code — Vessel or Plane — Date
Name — Age/Sex List Group Volume

Repository _____ ; Film number _____ ; Volume and page _____ ; Date researched _____
Copy of original made _____ ?; Researcher's Notes:

16 • *Documents of Our Ancestors*

ORDER FOR COPIES OF SHIP PASSENGER ARRIVAL RECORDS

Dear Researcher,

Before completing the form, please read this page for ordering instructions and general information about the records that can be ordered with this form. Mail order photocopying service using this form is available ONLY from *General Reference Branch (NNRG), National Archives and Records Administration, 7th and Pennsylvania Avenue NW., Washington, DC 20408.* For more information, please write to us at the address above.

IMPORTANT INFORMATION

WHAT WE HAVE: The National Archives has inbound Federal ship passenger arrival records dating back to 1820 for most east coast and gulf coast ports and a few lists dating back to 1800 for Philadelphia. Ship passenger lists in our custody are not complete. Fire, dampness, or other causes destroyed many records in the 19th century before the creating agencies transferred them to the National Archives. During the 19th century, no law required passenger arrival records to be kept for persons entering the United States by land from Canada or Mexico. No law required the keeping of outbound passenger lists.

WHAT WE CAN SEARCH: *Passenger Indexes:* We can search indexes if you supply the following information: full name of the passenger, port of entry, and approximate date of arrival. The following major indexes exist: Baltimore (1820-1952), Boston (1848-91 and 1902-20), New Orleans (1853-1952), New York (1820-46 and 1897-1948), Philadelphia (1800-1948), and minor ports (1820-74 and 1890-1924). *Unindexed Passenger Lists:* We cannot search these lists without more specific information than we require for index searches. To search unindexed passenger lists through 1892, you must supply port of entry, name of the vessel, approximate date of arrival, and the full name of the passenger. For those lists, we can also make a search with port of embarkation, exact date of arrival, port of entry, and the full name of the passenger. To search unindexed lists after 1892, we need the port of entry, the name of the vessel, the exact date of arrival, the full name of the passenger, and the names and ages of accompanying passengers, if any. PLEASE NOTE: There is no index for New York for the period 1847 through 1896 or for the period 1949 through the present.

ADDITIONAL INFORMATION: You may order copies of an entire passenger list by making a specific request. Write to the General Reference Branch at the address above. We will notify you of the cost. In addition, you or your representatives may search records that are too voluminous for the National Archives staff to search. We do not maintain a list of persons who do research for a fee. However, many researchers advertise their services in genealogical periodicals, usually available in libraries. *Naturalization (Citizenship) Records:* Naturalization records are separate from passenger arrival lists. The National Archives has copies of naturalization papers (1798-1906) for Massachusetts, New Hampshire, Rhode Island, and Maine and original records (1802-1926) for the District of Columbia. For information about citizenship granted elsewhere through September 26, 1906, write to the Federal, State, or municipal court that issued the naturalization. The Immigration and Naturalization Service, Washington, DC 20536 can furnish information on naturalizations that occurred after September 26, 1906.

INSTRUCTIONS FOR COMPLETING THIS FORM

Use a separate NATF Form 81 for each passenger arrival record. Remove this instruction sheet. Print your name (last, first, middle) and address in the block provided at the bottom of the form, which is your mailing label. The information must be legible on all copies. Keep the PINK copy of the form for your records. Mail the remaining three pages of the form to: *General Reference Branch (NNRG), National Archives and Records Administration, 7th and Pennsylvania Avenue NW., Washington, DC 20408.* Please allow 8 to 10 weeks for processing your order. **DO NOT SEND PAYMENT WITH THIS FORM.** When we search your order, we will make photocopies of records that relate to your request. For credit card orders, we will mail the copies immediately. For other type of orders, we will invoice you for the cost of these copies and hold them up to 45 days pending receipt of your payment.

NATIONAL ARCHIVES TRUST FUND BOARD   INSTRUCTIONS   NATF Form 81 (rev. 4-92)

A Selection of Reproducible Genealogy Forms and Tips for Using Them • 17

ORDER FOR COPIES OF SHIP PASSENGER ARRIVAL RECORDS

(See Instructions page before completing this form)

DATE RECEIVED *(NNRG)*

INDICATE BELOW THE METHOD OF PAYMENT PREFERRED.

☐ **CREDIT CARD** *(VISA or MasterCard)* for IMMEDIATE SHIPMENT of copies
Account Number: Exp. Date: Signature   Daytime Phone:

☐ **BILL ME** *(No credit card)*

IDENTIFICATION OF ENTRY

DATE OF ARRIVAL	FULL NAME OF PASSENGER *(Give last, first, and middle names)*	AGE	SEX
PORT OF ENTRY	NAMES OF MEMBERS OF IMMIGRANT FAMILY		
WHERE NATURALIZED *(if known)*			
SHIP NAME *(or Carrier Line)*			
PASSENGER'S COUNTRY OF ORIGIN			

NATIONAL ARCHIVES TRUST FUND BOARD   NATF Form 81 (rev. 4-92)

DO NOT WRITE BELOW - SPACE IS FOR OUR REPLY TO YOU

☐ **NO--We were unable to locate the record you requested above. No payment is required.**

MICROFILM PUBLICATION	ROLL	PAGE
RECORDS SEARCHED	SEARCHER	
		DATE SEARCHED

☐ A SEARCH WAS NOT MADE because the records you requested are not documented in our ship passenger arrival list records. Please see the reverse of this form. Also, please see the enclosed pamphlet for further information about our holdings.

☐ A SEARCH WAS NOT MADE because insufficient information was supplied. Please see the reverse of this form.

☐ A SEARCH WAS MADE BUT THE RECORD YOU REQUESTED ABOVE WAS NOT FOUND. Please see the reverse of this form.

☐ A SEARCH WAS MADE BUT THE EXACT RECORD YOU REQUESTED ABOVE WAS NOT FOUND. We found a record that may be the one you seek. Please see the reverse of this form.

☐ **YES--We located the record you requested above. We have made copies from the record for you. The cost for these copies is $10.**

MICROFILM PUBLICATION	ROLL	PAGE
SEARCHER		DATE SEARCHED
ARRIVAL DATE		
PORT		
SHIP		

Make your check or money order payable to NATIONAL ARCHIVES TRUST FUND. Do not send cash. Return this form and your payment in the enclosed envelope to:

NATIONAL ARCHIVES TRUST FUND
P.O. BOX 100221
ATLANTA, GA 30384-0221

PLEASE NOTE: We will hold these copies awaiting receipt of payment for only 45 days from the date completed, which is stamped below. After that time, you must submit another form to obtain photocopies of the record.

THIS IS YOUR MAILING LABEL

PRESS FIRMLY.

NAME (Last, First, MI)
STREET
CITY, STATE   ZIP CODE

B188611

INVOICE/REPLY COPY - DO NOT DETACH

Documents of Our Ancestors

Passenger Arrival Abstract

Name _____
Soundex _____

A. Index Card Information:

Name _____
Accompanied by _____,
Place of birth _____, Age (yrs/month) _____, Sex _____,
Marital status _____, Occupation _____, Read/write? _____,
Race _____.
Nationality/citizen of _____, Last permanent residence (town/country, etc.)
_____, Name/address of relative whence alien came
_____.
Ever in U.S.? _____, From _____, To _____, Where _____.
Passage paid by _____, Destination & name/address of relative joining in the U.S.
_____, Money shown $ _____,
Ever arrested/deported/excluded from admission? _____,
Head tax status _____, Height _____, Complexion _____,
Hair _____, Eyes _____, Distinguishing marks _____,
Seaport, date of landing, name of steamship, line:

Group-List-Volume

Repository _____; Film number _____; Volume and page _____; Date researched _____; Copy of original made _____? Researcher's Notes:

B. Passenger Manifest Information:

Vessel name _____, Shipping Line _____, Volume _____,
Departing from (port) _____, departure date _____,
Arriving at (port) _____, arrival date _____,
Page no. _____, List or line no. _____,
Name in full _____.
Age (yrs/mos.) _____, Sex _____, Race or people _____,
Married/Single _____, Citizen of _____,
Calling/Occupation _____, Able to read? _____, Write? _____,
Nationality/native country/province _____, Last permanent residence
(province/city/town) _____, Location of compartment space _____,
No. of pieces of baggage _____, Transient or intending protracted sojourn _____?
Date and cause of death _____. Name and address of relative in country from which
alien departed _____, Ever in U.S. (when/where) _____?

A Selection of Reproducible Genealogy Forms and Tips for Using Them • 19

Port of landing _____, Seaport of destination in U.S._____,
Final U.S. destination (state/city/town) _____, Ticket to final destination
_____? Passage paid by _____, Money shown $_____,
Going to join a relative (name/address) _____,
Intending to return home_____? Length of intended stay_____? Intending to become a citizen_____?
Ever in prison/supported by charity _____? Ever arrested,/deported/excluded from admission _____? Polygamist _____? Anarchist_____? Believe in violent overthrow of U.S. govt_____? Contract laborer_____?
Previously deported_____? Condition of health_____,
Deformed or crippled_____? Height _____, Color_____,
Complexion _____, Hair _____, Eyes _____, Marks _____,
Place of birth _____, Mother tongue_____, Subject of what country_____, Religion_____.
Others traveling with this person (complete separate forms):

Held for special inquiry _____?

| Repository _____; Film number _____; Volume and page_____; Date researched _____; Copy of original made _____? Researcher's Notes: |

20 • *Documents of Our Ancestors*

Customs List of Passengers
1 January 1883 – 16 June 1897, page 1

Master_____ Vessel_____ Manifest No._____ Date of Embarkation_____ Date of Arrival_____

List No.	Names	Age		Sex	Calling or Occupation	Native Country	Intended Destination (state or country)
		Years	Months				

A Selection of Reproducible Genealogy Forms and Tips for Using Them

Customs List of Passengers
1 January 1883 – 16 June 1897, page 2

Location of Compartment or space occupied (forward, amidships, or aft)	Number of Pieces of Baggage	Transient in transit, or intending protracted sojourn	Port of Embarkation	Date and Cause of Death	(repealed) Able to	
					Read	Write

Repository _____ ; Film number _____ ; Volume and page _____ ;
Date researched _____ ; Copy of original made _____ ?; Researcher's Notes:

Manifest of Alien Passengers
16 June 1897 – 5 September 1903, page 1

Vessel ____ Date embarked ____ Port embarked ____ Date arrived in N.Y. ____ Volume ____ Group ____

First class ____
Second class ____
Steerage ____

1	2	3		4	5	6	7		8	9	10	11	12	13
No. on List	Name in Full	Age		Sex	Married or Single	Calling or Occupation	Able to		Nationality	Last Residence	Seaport of Destination in U.S.	Final Destination in U.S. (state, city, or town)	Whether having a ticket?	By whom was passage paid?
		Months	Years				Read	Write						

A Selection of Reproducible Genealogy Forms and Tips for Using Them

Manifest of Alien Passengers
16 June 1897 -- 5 September 1903, page 2

14	14	16	17	18	19	20	21	Supplement to Manifest of Alien Passengers					
Having $30, if not, how much	Ever been in U.S.? If so, when and where?	Going to join relative? If so, name & address of relative	Ever in prison, almshouse, or supported by charity? Which?	Polygamist?	Contract laborer?	Condition of health? Mental & physical?	Deformed or crippled? Nature & cause?	Color	Nativity		Mother tongue (language or dialect)	Subject of what country?	Religion
									Country	Province			

Repository _____; Film number _____; Volume and page _____; Date researched _____; Copy of original made _____
_____?; Researcher's Notes:

Manifest of Alien Passengers
5 September 1903 – 30 June 1907, page 1

Vessel _____ Date embarked _____ Port embarked _____ Date arrived in N.Y. _____ Volume _____ Group _____

First class _____
Second class _____
Steerage _____

1	2	3		4	5	6	7		8	9	10	11	12	13	14
No. on List	Name in Full	Age		Sex	Married or Single	Calling or Occupation	Able to		Nationality (Country of last permanent residence)	Race or People	Last residence (province, city, or town)	Final destination (state, city or town)	Whether having a ticket?	By whom was passage paid?	Whether in possession of $50. If not, how much?
		Years	Months				Read	Write							

A Selection of Reproducible Genealogy Forms and Tips for Using Them

Manifest of Alien Passengers
5 September 1903 – 30 June 1907, page 2

15	16	17	18	19	20	21	22	Attached Slip (after 29 June 1906)						
								Personal Description						Place of Birth
								Height		Comp-lexion	Color of		Marks of Identi-fication	
Ever in U.S.? If so, when and where?	Going to join relative? If so, name & address of relative.	Even in prison, almshouse, or supported by charity? Which?	Polyga-mist?	Anar-chist?	Contract laborer?	Condition of health? Mental & physical?	Deformed or crippled? Nature & cause?	Feet	Inches		Hair	Eyes		

Repository _____; Film number _____; Volume and page _____;
Date researched _____; Copy of original made _____; Researcher's Notes:

Manifest of Alien Passengers
1 July 1907 -- 4 December 1913, page 1

Vessel_____ Date embarked_____ Port embarked_____ Date arrived in N.Y._____ Volume_____ Group_____

First class_____
Second class_____
Steerage_____

1	2		3		4	5	6	7		8	9	10		11	12	
No. on List	Name in Full		Age		Sex	Married or Single	Calling or Occupation	Able to		Nationality (Country which citizen or subject)	Race or People	Last permanent residence		Name and address of nearest relative or friend in country whence alien came	Final Destination	
	Family Name	Given Name	Years	Months				Read	Write			Country	City or Town		State	City or Town

A Selection of Reproducible Genealogy Forms and Tips for Using Them

Manifest of Alien Passengers
1 July 1907 – 4 December 1913, page 2

13	14	15	16	17			18	19	20	21
No. on List	Whether having a ticket	By whom was passage paid?	Whether in possession of $50. If not, how much?	Ever in U.S.?			Going to join relative? If so, name & address of relative	Ever in prison or almshouse?	Polygamist?	Anarchist?
				Yes/No	If yes—					
					Years?	Where?				

Repository _____ ; Film number _____ ; Volume and page _____ ;
Date researched _____ ; Copy of original made _____ ?; Researcher's Notes:

Manifest of Alien Passengers
July 1907 – 4 December 1913, page 3

22	23	24	Supplemental (after 29 June 1906)					
			25 Height		26 Comp-lexion	27 Color of		28 Marks of Identi-fication	29 Place of birth	
Contract laborer?	Health condition?	Deformed or crippled?	Feet	Inches		Hair	Eyes		Country	City or Town

Repository _____; Film number _____; Volume and page _____;
Date researched _____; Copy of original made _____?; Researcher's Notes:

A Selection of Reproducible Genealogy Forms and Tips for Using Them

List or Manifest of Alien Passengers
5 December 1913 -- 31 August 1917, page 1

Vessel _____ Date embarked _____ Port embarked _____ Date arrived in N.Y. _____ Volume _____ Group _____

First class _____
Second class _____
Steerage _____

1	2		3		4	5	6	7		8	9	10	
No. on List	Name in Full		Age		Sex	Married/ Single	Calling or Occupation	Able to:		Nationality (Country which citizen or subject)	Race or People	Last Permanent Residence	
	Family Name	Given Name	Years	Months				Read	Write			Country	City or Town

List or Manifest of Alien Passengers
5 December 1913 -- 31 August 1917, page 2

11	13		14	15	16	17			18
Name & address of nearest relative or friend in country whence alien came	Final Destination		Whether having a ticket	By whom was passage paid?	Whether in possession of $50. If not, how much?	Ever in U.S.?	If yes,		Going to join relative? If so, name & address of relative
	State	City or Town				Yes/ No	Years?	Where?	

List or Manifest of Alien Passengers
5 December 1913 -- 31 August 1917, page 3

19	20	21	22	23	24	Supplemental (after 29 June 1906)							
						25		26	27		28	29	
Ever in prison or alms-house?	Poly-gamist?	Anar-chist?	Contract laborer?	Health condition?	Deformed or crippled?	Height		Complexion	Color of		Marks of identifi-cation	Place of Birth	
						Feet	Inches		Hair	Eyes		Country	City or Town

Repository: _____; Film number _____; Volume and page _____; Date researched _____; Copy of original made _____
_____?, Researcher's Notes:

List or Manifest of Alien Passengers
1 September 1917 -- After 31 December 1920, page 1

Vessel_____ Date embarked_____ Port embarked_____ Date arrived in N.Y._____ Volume_____ Group_____

First class____
Second class____
Steerage____

1	2	3		4		5	6	7	8		9	10
No. on List	Head-tax status	Name in Full		Age		Sex	Married-Single	Calling or Occupation	Able to		Nationality (Country which citizen or subject)	Race or People
		Family Name	Given Name	Years	Months				Read	Write		

A Selection of Reproducible Genealogy Forms and Tips for Using Them

List or Manifest of Alien Passengers
1 September 1917 -- After 31 December 1920, page 2

11 Last Permanent Residence		12 Name & address of nearest relative or friend in country whence alien came	13 Final Destination		15 Whether having a ticket?	16 By whom was passage paid?	17 Whether in possession of $50. If not, how much?	18 Ever in U.S.?			19 Going to join relative? If so, name & address of relative
Country	City or Town		State	City or Town				Yes/ No	If yes--		
									Years?	Where?	

List or Manifest of Alien Passengers
1 September 1917 -- After 31 December 1920, page 3

20			21	22	23	24	25	26	27	28
Purpose of coming to the U.S.										
Whether alien intends to return to country whence he came after temporarily working in U.S.	Length of time alien intends to remain in U.S.	Whether alien intends to become a citizen of U.S.	Ever in prison or almshouse	Poly-gamist?	Anar-chist?	Whether person believes in the violent overthrow of U.S. Govt.	Contract Laborer?	Whether alien had been previously deported within one year	Health condition?	Deformed or crippled?

A Selection of Reproducible Genealogy Forms and Tips for Using Them

List or Manifest of Alien Passengers
1 September 1917 – After 31 December 1920, page 4

29 Height		30 Complexion	31 Color of		32 Marks of Identi-fication	33 Place of Birth	
Feet	Inches		Hair	Eyes		Country	City or Town

Repository _____; Film number _____; Volume and page _____;
Date researched _____; Copy of original made _____?; Researcher's Notes:

36 • *Documents of Our Ancestors*

World War I Draft Registrations

Forms Provided

   A. *World War I [Draft] Registration Card Request*
   B. *World War I Draft Registration Card*

What Records Are Available

Three draft registrations took place between June 1917 and September 1918 during which about 24 million men were registered by some 4600 draft boards—each covering about 30,000 people. As shown on the cards, these records can be of great genealogical value in providing birth dates, birth places, name of wife, and much more.

Over the three registration periods, all men born between 1873 and 1900 were required to register, whether citizens or aliens. For men born between 1886 and 1897, this form provides the exact place of birth including town, province, or county, U.S. or foreign country.

The recording form is a replica of a form that varied somewhat over the three periods of its use (e.g., one version asked for both the age of the individual as well as date of birth; another asked for date of birth only). This version includes spaces for the all the information requested.

Where to Find Them

A substantial but incomplete set can be searched at the Family History Library and its branches. Catalog reference: United States–Military Records—World War, 1914–1918. The originals are located at the National Archives, Southeast Region, 1557 St. Joseph Avenue, East Point, GA 30344 and can be searched using the enclosed form.

What You Need Before You Search

   - Name of city (see instructions on request form)
   - Full legal name
   - Approximate age
   - For larger cities or counties, address or neighborhood

Tips

- The microfilmed copies of the cards are filed in alphabetical order, by state, city or county, and draft board number (except for Connecticut, Massachusetts, and Rhode Island which are arranged by divisions and counties).
- The lists are not indexed. The researcher must know at least the name of the city where the person was living in 1917–18. Smaller cities had only a few draft boards so an in-person search should be fairly easy.
- For the larger cities listed on the reverse of the Request form, the researcher must have at least some idea where the person was living to narrow the search to one or a few draft boards. Maps showing draft board boundaries of some of the largest cities are on a microfilm at the Family History Library (film number 1,498,803). Qualifiers and details on how to use these maps are in the Meshenberg article listed below.
- As with many other lists, the accuracy of the alphabetizing varies. Sometimes whole groups of cards are out of order. If you cannot find a person you are reasonably sure should be in the particular draft board list, check for misalphabetized cards.

Additional Help

Jewish Gen InfoFile, "WWI Draft Registration Cards," <http://www.jewishgen.org>.

Meshenberg, Michael J., "Searching for World War I Draft Registration Records," *Avotaynu*, vol. XI, no. 1, Spring 1994.

"World War I Draft Registrations," *Avotaynu,* vol. IX, no. 1, Spring 1993.

National Archives—Southeast Region

1557 St. Joseph Avenue   East Point, Georgia 30344

WORLD WAR I REGISTRATION CARD REQUEST

ATTENTION:

More than 24,000,000 World War I Selective Service records are on file at our Center. They are filed by state and by draft board. To search this large file, we must have the full name of the person and their city and/or county at the time of registration. For the cities on the reverse side, a home and street address or other specific location information (such as ward) is required.

Please complete this form and return it to us. For each card required, complete a separate request form and enclose $6.00. Make check payable to: NATIONAL ARCHIVES TRUST FUND.

REGISTRANT DATA   (Completed by Requestor)
Full name of Registrant   Birthdate

Home Address at time of registration (complete)   Birthplace (complete)

Draft Board Location (city, county, street address)   Registration Date

---

Name of Wife or nearest relative at time of registration   Occupation

---

SIGNATURE OF REQUESTOR: DATE:

REQUESTOR'S NAME AND ADDRESS (Please Print Clearly)

(PLEASE READ REVERSE SIDE FOR CITIES REQUIRING SPECIFIC INFORMATION)

CITIES FOR WHICH A STREET ADDRESS OR OTHER SPECIFIC INFORMATION IS REQUIRED

CALIFORNIA
Los Angeles
San Francisco

DISTRICT OF COLUMBIA
Washington

GEORGIA
Atlanta

ILLINOIS
Chicago

INDIANA
Indianapolis

KENTUCKY
Louisville

LOUISIANA
New Orleans

MARYLAND
Baltimore

MASSACHUSETTS
Boston

MINNESOTA
Minneapolis
St. Paul

MISSOURI
Kansas City
St. Louis

NEW JERSEY
Jersey City
Newark

NEW YORK
Albany
Buffalo
New York City
Syracuse

OHIO
Cincinnati
Cleveland

PENNSYLVANIA
Luzerne County
Philadelphia
Pittsburg

RHODE ISLAND
Providence

WASHINGTON
Seattle

WISCONSIN
Milwaukee

DRAFT REGISTRATIONS WERE HELD AS FOLLOWS:

1. June 5, 1917. All men between the ages of 21 and 31 years of age were required to register.

2. June 5, 1918. All men who had become 21 years of age since June 5, 1917. A supplemental registration was held on August 24, 1918, at which time were men who had become 21 years of age since June 5, 1918 were required to register.

3. September 12, 1918. This registration provided for the registration of all men between the ages of 18 and 21, and 31 to 45 years of age. This was the third and last World War I registration.

WWI Draft Registration Card, p. 1

REGISTRATION CARD

Serial Number				Order Number	

1. _____
   (Given name)   (Middle name)   (Last name)

2. Permanent Home Address
   _____
   (no.)   (street or R.F.D. No.)   (City or town)   (County)   (State)

3. Age in Years _____ 4. Date of Birth _____
   (month)   (day)   (year)

5. Are you (1) a natural-born citizen, (2) a naturalized citizen, (3) an alien, (4) or have you declared your intention (specify which)? _____

6. Where were you born? _____
   (Town)   (State)   (Nation)

7. If not a citizen, of what country are you a subject? _____

8. What is your present trade occupation, or office? _____

9. By whom employed? _____
   Where employed? _____

10. Have you a father, mother, wife, child under 12, or a sister or brother under 12, wholely dependent on you for support (specify which)? _____

11. Married or single (specify which)? _____   Race (specify which) _____

12. Name and address of nearest relative: _____

13. What military service have you had? Rank _____ ; Branch _____
    Years _____ ; Nation or State _____

14. Do you claim exemption from draft (specify grounds)? _____

I affirm that I have verified above answers and think they are true.

_____
(Signature or mark)

WWI Draft Registration Card, p. 2

REGISTRAR'S REPORT

DESCRIPTION OF REGISTRANT

HEIGHT			BUILD			COLOR OF EYES	COLOR OF HAIR
Tall	Medium	Short	Slender	Medium	Heavy		
15	16	17	18	19	20	21	22

23. Has person lost arm, leg, hand, eye or is he otherwise disabled (specify)?
_____
_____

24. I certify that my answers are true, that the person registered has signed his signature, that I have witnessed his signature, and that all of his statements of which I have knowledge are true, except as follows:
_____
_____

_____
(signature of registrar)

Precinct: _____
City or County: _____
State: _____

_____
(Date of Registration)

_____
(No. of Board or Division)

Repository _____; Film number _____; Volume and page _____;
Date researched _____; Copy of original made _____?; Researcher's Notes:

Naturalization Records and Alien Registration Records

Forms Provided

    A. *U.S. Department of Justice, Immigration and Naturalization Service, Freedom of Information/Privacy Act Request (Form G-639)*
    B. *Naturalization Abstract*
    C. *Declaration of Intention, Form 2202: September 27, 1906 – July 1, 1929*
    D. *Declaration of Intention, Form 2202 L-A: July 1, 1929 – January 13, 1941*
    E. *Declaration of Intention, Form N-315: January 13, 1941 – (voluntary after December 24, 1952)*
    F. *Old Law (pre-1906) Petition for Naturalization*
    G. *Petition for Naturalization, Form 2204: 1913 – June 30, 1929*
    H. *Petition for Naturalization, Form 2204 L-A: July 1, 1929 – January 13, 1941*
    I. *Petition for Naturalization, Form N-405: January 1, 1941 –*
    J. *Alien Registration Form (Form AR-2)*

What Records Are Available

Naturalization records. Declarations, petitions, and certificates, provide a wealth of valuable genealogical data. Although the records are public documents, finding the court in which someone became naturalized often is no easy task. The records may be at the court, a National Archives branch, the National Archives in Washington, D.C., or the Family History Library. Some are indexed, while others are not. Few generalizations can be made. After narrowing the search to a few possibilities it is best to learn as much as possible about the holdings of various repositories before conducting an in-person search or spending money.

Alien Registration Forms. Beginning in 1941, all aliens (non-U.S. citizens) were required to register with the Immigration and Naturalization Service under the 1940 Alien Registration Act. The registration form used, AR-2, contains information similar to naturalization petitions and is of similar genealogical benefit. Copies are available only from INS in Washington and can be requested by filing the Freedom of Information request form, G-639.

Where to Find Them

For individuals naturalized after September 27, 1906, or for alien registration information, send Form G-639 to FOIA/PA Unit, Immigration and Naturalization Service, Room 5114, 425 Eye Street, N.W., Washington, DC 20536. (202) 514-1554. For naturalizations before that date, researchers must obtain records from the court in which the naturalization occurred. Many records also are available from NARA field offices. Alien registration information is available only by mail from INS.

What You Need Before You Search

By mail:

    INS maintains an index to all naturalizations that occurred during the years 1906–56, but it is not available for public use. The Request Form must be completed to initiate a search for either naturalization or alien registration records. The form indicates what data must be provided but a search may be successful if at least the following is provided:

    – Full legal name.
    – Approximate age.

A Selection of Reproducible Genealogy Forms and Tips for Using Them • 43

In person:

> If searching in person, for example at a NARA branch or FHC, the name of the court must be known because all records are filed by court. (There are consolidated indexes for New York City courts 1795–1906, in the FHL catalog under New York, New York (City) - Naturalization and Citizenship - Indexes, and for New England 1791–1906 cataloged under United States, New England—Naturalization and Citizenship—Indexes.) Additional information, such as occupation, is helpful if the name is relatively common.

Tips

General information on finding a naturalization record:
- If naturalized before 1906, try the court, FHL, or a National Archives branch.
- After 1906, records are obtainable either from INS (see form) or the court. Locating the court of naturalization is often a hit or miss proposition. If the person was living in New York during the 1925 New York State Census, the Census usually (but not always) provides the name of the court and year. Voter registration records are another source (see below).

Request Form:
- Check the FOIA box.
- If looking for people who were naturalized after 1906, on the FOIA form request the COMPLETE file including: "Social Security number, passport, Certificate of Naturalization, Petition for Naturalization, Declaration of Intent, birth certificate in original language with English translation, medical and health certificate, letter to the U.S. consulate, and other relevant documents in the file."
- INS will usually acknowledge a request within 6–8 weeks and provide a "control number." But the reply with the results of the search can take 1½ years or more. Because of the slow response time, it is better to first try the court where the naturalization took place, the local INS regional office, or do it yourself at the local Family History Center.
- Many of the twelve NARA branches have microfilm records of naturalizations that occurred in the federal courts in that region. The fee (without needing the form) usually is only $6.00, not the $25.00 typically charged by NARA headquarters in Washington, and they tend to reply much more quickly.

Naturalization Abstract:
- This form is generic; there have been numerous variations in both petitions and declarations of intent, and many of the headings may not apply. The photocopies of the actual forms show what information can be expected in a given year.
- Indexing systems are highly variable and frequently provide insufficient information to identify particular individuals with certainty. A researcher may have to obtain several records to find the right one.
- Keep a record of index information, especially if the date and place of obtaining index information is different from that of the actual record. Index information varies considerably—sometimes it is very detailed (as in the consolidated index for all pre-1906 New York City courts), sufficient to specifically identify the person being sought, or very obscure, with only numbers that don't seem to equate with anything recognizable. Make sure you copy down everything exactly, especially if the record is being requested by mail. You may not know what the numbers mean, but the clerks will.
- Very little information is included in pre-1906 naturalizations; much more is provided later.
- Abstracts for both declarations and petitions are provided on the form; there is usually much more information on the petition but if you have both, copy both. Sometimes information provided is different either because the information has changed (e.g., petitioner has moved or new children were born) or because it's just different.
- Reproductions of declaration forms are provided from 1906 on, and for petitions from pre-1906 (Old Law) through 1941. These forms can be used to copy information directly off a microfilm for the appropriate year.
- The Family History Library has indexes to the naturalizations for many courts. They are cataloged under:

44 • *Documents of Our Ancestors*

[State, Locality] - Naturalization and Citizenship. It has fewer records. You will need to provide the index information to the court of record (before 1906), or the National Archives (after 1906), to obtain copies of the records.

Additional Help

Goldstein, Irene Saunders, "Greater Access to U.S. Naturalization Records," *Avotaynu,* vol. VIII, no. 1, Spring 1992, p. 41.

Guzik, *Genealogical Resources in the New York Metropolitan Area,* provides information on all locations in the New York area that have naturalization records.

JewishGen InfoFile, "JewishGen FAQ—Frequently Asked Questions," section 12, Naturalization Records, <http://www.jewishgen.org>, April 1996.

Luft, Edward David, "Recording Post-1906 Naturalizations in Washington, DC," *Avotaynu,* vol. X, no. 3, Fall 1994.

National Archives Trust Fund Board, *Guide to Genealogical Research in the National Archives* (Washington: NARA, Revised 1985). Chart 3 contains a detailed, state-by-state listing of the federal court naturalization records and the indexes to them available in the 12 regional archive branches.

_____, *Federal Court Records: A Select Catalog of National Archives Microfilm Publications,* 1987.

Neagles, James C. and Lila Lee Neagles. *Locating Your Immigrant Ancestors: A Guide to Naturalization Records* (Logan, Utah: Everton Publishers, Inc. 1975; revised 1986).

Newman, John J., *American Naturalization Process and Procedures 1790–1983* (Indianapolis, IN: Family History Section, Indiana Historical Society, 1985).

Sack, Sallyann Amdur, "Recent Acquisitions of the LDS (Mormon) Family History Library," *Avotaynu,* vol. IX, no. 1, Spring 1993.

Your Right to Federal Records: Questions and Answers on the Freedom of Information Act and the Privacy Act, <gopher://gopher.gsa.gov:70/00/staff/pa/cic/misc/other/foia.txt>, 1992.

U.S. Department of Justice
Immigration and Naturalization Service

OMB No. 1115-0087
Freedom of Information/Privacy Act Request

START HERE - Please Type or Print and read instructions on the reverse before completing this form.

1. Type of Request: *(Check appropriate box)*   a. ☐ Freedom of Information Act *(FOIA) (complete all items except 6)*
   b. ☐ Privacy Act *(PA) (Item 6 **Must** be completed in addition to all other applicable items)*   c. ☐ Amendment *(PA only)*

2. List below, the name and telephone number of the person to whom the information should be released. By my signature, I consent to the following *(check applicable boxes)*:
   a. ☐ Pay all costs incurred for search, duplication and review of materials up to $25.00, when applicable. *(see reverse)*
   b. ☐ Allow the person name below to see *(my record/a portion)* **(Specify)** _____
      (Consent is required for records for USC and Lawful Permanent Residents)
   c. ☐ Proof of Death is attached for deceased subject *(obituary or death certificate)*

   Name of person authorized to see record: Signature of person giving consent:

   Name: Day time phone number: (   ) -

   Address *(street number and name)*:   Apt. No.:

   City: State: Zip Code:

3. Action Request *(check one)*:   a. ☐ Copy   b. ☐ In-person Review

4. **Information needed to search for record(s):**

   Specific information, document(s), or record(s) desired. *(Identify by name, date subject matter and location of information)*
   _____
   _____

   Purpose *(optional)* *(You are not required to state the purpose for your request. However, doing so may assist the INS in locating the records needed to respond to you.)*
   _____
   _____

5. Data **NEEDED** on **SUBJECT** of Record *(*If not provided records may not be located)*:

*Family Name:	Given Name:	Middle Name:
*Other names used, *if any*:	*Name at time of Entry in U.S.:	I-94 Admissions#:
*Alien Registration #: *Petition#:	*Country of Birth:	*Date of Birth or Age:

   Names of other Family Members that may appear on requested record *(i.e., daughter, son, spouse)*:

Country of Origin:	Port of Entry into U.S.:	Date of Entry:
Manner of Entry *(air, sea, land)*:	Mode of Travel *(name of carrier)*:	SSAN:
*Name on Naturalization Certification:	Certificate #:	Naturalization Date:
Address at time of Naturalization:		Court and Location:

6. Verification of Subject's Identity: *(See reverse for explanation)* *(check one)*:
   a. ☐ In person with ID   b. ☐ Notarized Affidavit of Identity   c. ☐ Other (Specify)_____

   Signature of Requester: Date: Telephone Number: (   ) -

Form G-639 (Rev. 10-30-92) N   *(See Reverse)*

U.S. Department of Justice
Immigration and Naturalization Service

OMB No. 1115-0087
Freedom of Information Privacy Act Request

NOTARY (normally needed from individuals who are the subject of the record sought (see below)

subscribed and sworn to before me this _____ day of _____ ,19 _____ .

(include Notary Seal or Stamp in this Space)

Signature of Notary _____
My Commission Expires _____

INSTRUCTIONS
PLEASE READ ALL INSTRUCTIONS CAREFULLY BEFORE COMPLETING THIS FORM.
Applicants making false statements are subject to criminal penalties [Pub. L. 93--579.88 stat. (5 U.S.C. 552a (i)(3)].

Do Not Use This Form For The Following Reasons:
(1) Determine status of pending applications - call nearest INS office. (2) Consular notification of visa petition approval - use Form I-824. (3) Return of Original documents - Use Form G-884. (4) For records of naturalization prior to Sept 27, 1906 - write to the clerk of court where naturalization occurred. (5) INS arrivals prior to 1891, except for arrivals at the port of NY, which began as of June 16, 1897 - write to the National Archives.

How to Submit a Request.
Person requesting a search for **access to INS records** under the Freedom of Information or Privacy Acts may submit the completed application to the INS office nearest the applicant's place of residence. Requests may be submitted in person or by mail. If an application is mailed, the envelope should be clearly marked *"Freedom of information" or "Privacy Act Information Request."*

Information Needed to Search for Records
Please Note: Failure to provide complete and specific information as requested in item 5, may result in a delay in processing or inability to locate the records or information requested.

Verification of Identity in Person.
Requesters appearing in person for access to their records may identify themselves by showing a document bearing a photograph *(such as an Alien Registration Card, form I-551, Citizen Identification Card, Naturalization Certificate, or passport) or two items which bear their name and address (such as driver's license and voter's registration).*

Verification of Identity by Mail.
Requesters wanting **access to their records** shall identify themselves by name, current address, date and place of birth and alien or employee identification number. A notarized example of their signatures must also be provided (this form or a DOJ Form 361, Certification of Identity, may be used for this purpose).

Verification of Identity of Guardians.
Parents or legal guardians must establish their own identity as parents or legal guardians and the identity of the child or other person being represented.

Authorization or Consent.
Other parties requesting nonpublic information about an individual usually must have the consent of that individual on Form G-639 or by authorizing letter, together with appropriate verification of identity of the record subject. Notarized consent is required from a record subject who is a lawful permanent resident or U.S. Citizen, and for access to certain Legalization files

Fees.
Except for commercial requesters, the first 100 pages of reproduction and two hours of search time will be furnished without charge. For requests processed under the Privacy Act, there may be a fee of $.10 per page for photocopy duplication. For requests processed under the Freedom of Information Act, there may be a fee for quarter hours of time spent for searches and for review of records. Search fees are at the following rates; $2.25 clerical; $4.50 professional/computer operator; and $7.50 managerial. Other costs for searches and duplication will be charged at the actual direct cost. Fees will only be charged if the aggregate amount of fees for searches, copy and/or review is more than $8.00. If the total anticipated fees amount to more than $250.00, or the same requester has failed to pay fees in the past, an advance deposit may be requested.

Fee waivers or reductions may be requested for a request that clearly will benefit the public and is not primarily in the personal or commercial interest of the requester. Such request's should include a justification.

Manner of Submission of Fees When Required.
Do not send cash. Fees must be submitted in the exact amount. When requested to do so, submit a check or a United States Postal money order (or, if application is submitted from outside the United States, remittance may be made by bank international money order or foreign draft drawn on a financial institution in the United States) made payable to the "Immigration and Naturalization Service," in United States currency. An Applicant residing in the U.S. Virgin Islands shall make his remittance payable to "Commissioner of Finance of the Virgin Islands," and, if residing in Guam, to "Treasurer, Guam."

A charge of $5.00 will be imposed if a check in payment of a fee is not honored by the bank on which it is drawn. Every remittance will be accepted subject to collection.

Privacy Act Statement.
Authority to collect this information is contained in Title 5 U.S.C. 552 and 552a. The purpose of the collection is to enable INS to locate applicable records and to respond to requests made under the Freedom of Information and Privacy Acts.

Routine Uses.
Information will be used to comply with requests for information under the Acts; information to other agencies for referrals consultations and answer subsequent inquiries concerning specific requests.

Effect of Not Providing Requested Information.
Furnishing the information requested on this form is voluntary. However, failure to furnish the information may result in the inability of INS to comply with a request when compliance will violate other policies or laws.

General Information
The Freedom of Information Act (5 U.S.C. 552) allows requesters to have access to Federal Agency records, except those which have been exempted by the Act.

The Privacy Act 1974. (5 U.SC. 552a), with certain exceptions, permits individuals (United States citizens or permanent resident aliens) to gain access to information pertaining to themselves in Federal agency records, to have a copy made of all or any part thereof, to correct or amend such records, and permit individuals to make requests concerning what records pertaining to themselves are collected, maintained, used or disseminated. The Act also prohibits disclosure of individuals' records without their written consent, except under certain circumstances.

Public Report Burden for this collection is estimated to average 15 minutes per response, including the time for reviewing instructions, searching existing data sources gathering and maintaining the data needed, and completing and reviewing the collection of information. Send comments regarding this burden estimated or any other aspect of this collection of information, including suggestions for reducing this burden , to: U.S. Department of Justice, Immigration and Naturalization Service, Policy Directives and Instructions Branch (HQPDIB), Washington, DC 20536; and to the Office of Management and Budget, Paperwork Reduction Project: OMB No. 1115-0087; Washington, DC 20503.

Name_____
Soundex_____

Naturalization Abstract

A. Declaration of Intention

Declaration No. _____.
Name of Court _____.
Declarer's Name _____.
Age _____, Sex _____, Occupation _____, Color _____,
Complexion _____, Height _____, Weight _____, Color of hair _____, Color of eyes _____, Other distinctive visible marks_____.
Race_____, Nationality_____.
Born in _____ On (date) _____.
Now residing at _____.
Emigrated from _____, On the vessel_____,
Last foreign residence _____;
Allegiance renounced to _____.
Port of arrival _____,
State/territory_____.
Date of arrival_____, Name used on emigration_____.
Married? _____. Name of wife/husband_____,
Married on (date) _____, At (city/town, state/country)_____,
Spouse born at (city/town, state/country)_____, On (date)_____,
Entered the United State at (city/town, state)_____,
On (date)_____, for permanent residence
and now resides at (city/town, state/country)_____.
I have_____ children. Names, date and place of birth, and residence of each child is:
_____
_____
_____
_____

Previous declaration of intention: Number_____, On (date)_____,
At (city/town, state, court) _____.
Date of oath _____.

Repository _____; Film number _____; Volume and page_____; Date researched _____; Copy of original made _____? Researcher's Notes:

48 • *Documents of Our Ancestors*

Name _____

Naturalization Abstract

B. Petition for Naturalization

Petition Number _____.
Name of Court _____.
Petitioner's Name _____.
Residence _____.
Occupation _____, Age _____, Date of birth _____,
Place of birth _____, Sex _____, Color _____,
Complexion _____, Color of eyes _____, Color of hair _____,
Height _____, Weight _____, Visible distinctive marks _____,
Race _____, Present nationality _____.
Date of declaration of intention _____, Place of declaration _____,
Court of declaration _____.

Married? _____, Name of wife or husband _____,
Date of marriage _____, Place of marriage _____,
Birthplace of spouse _____, Birth date of spouse _____,
Entered the U.S. at _____, Date of entry _____,
Present residence _____,
Date of naturalization _____, Place of naturalization _____,
Certificate number _____, Became a citizen by _____.
Number of children _____, Names, date and place of birth, and residence of each child is:
_____
_____
_____
_____
_____

Last place of foreign residence _____.
Emigrated from _____, Arrived at _____,
Name used at arrival _____,
Date of entry _____, Vessel _____ (Is Department of Labor
certificate of arrival attached _____? Filed on (date) _____.)
Renounce allegiance to _____.
Years of continuous residence in the U.S. _____, Since _____.
Continuously resided in the State of _____, Since _____.
Previous petition _____? If yes, number, date, place, court, action taken:

Petition to change name to _____.

A Selection of Reproducible Genealogy Forms and Tips for Using Them • 49

Since entering the U.S., I have____ been absent from the U.S. for a period of 6 months or longer:

DEPARTED FROM THE UNITED STATES   RETURNED TO THE UNITED STATES
Port   Date   Vessel   Port   Date   Vessel

Witnesses names, occupations, addresses:

Known petitioner since _____.

Court _____, date witnessed _____,
Date of Oath of Allegiance _____.
Certificate number _____.

Repository _____; Film number _____; Volume and page_____; Date researched _____; Copy of original made _____? Researcher's Notes:

50 • *Documents of Our Ancestors*

Declaration of Intention, Form 2202: September 27, 1906 – July 1, 1929

ORIGINAL

UNITED STATES OF AMERICA

Department of Commerce and Labor
BUREAU OF IMMIGRATION AND NATURALIZATION
DIVISION OF NATURALIZATION

DECLARATION OF INTENTION
(Invalid for all purposes seven years after the date hereof)

.... } ss: In the .... Court
.... of ....

I, ..., aged .... years,

occupation ...., do declare on oath / affirm that my personal

description is: Color .... complexion ...., height ..... feet ..... inches,

weight .... pounds, color of hair ...., color of eyes ....

other visible distinctive marks ....

...............................; I was born in ....

..................................., on the .... day of ...., anno

Domini 1........; I now reside at ....

I emigrated to the United States of America from ....

on the vessel* ....; my last

foreign residence was ....

It is my bona fide intention to renounce forever all allegiance and fidelity to any foreign

prince, potentate, state, or sovereignty, and particularly to ....

...., of which I am now a citizen/subject; I

arrived at the port of ...., in the

State
Territory of .... on or about the .... day
District

of ...., anno Domini 1........; I am not an anarchist; I am not a

polygamist nor a believer in the practice of polygamy; and it is my intention in good faith

to become a citizen of the United States of America and to permanently reside therein:

SO HELP ME GOD.

....
(Original signature of declarant.)

Subscribed and sworn to / affirmed before me this ....

[SEAL.] day of ...., anno Domini 19........

....

Clerk of the .... Court.

By ...., ... Clerk.

*If the alien arrived otherwise than by vessel, the character of conveyance or name of transportation company should be given.

11—2626

Repository _____; Film number _____; Volume and page _____;
Date researched _____; Copy of original made _____?; Researcher's Notes:

A Selection of Reproducible Genealogy Forms and Tips for Using Them • 51

Declaration of Intention, Form 2202 L-A: July 1, 1929 – January 13, 1941

ORIGINAL

No. ....

UNITED STATES OF AMERICA

DECLARATION OF INTENTION
(Invalid for all purposes seven years after the date hereof)

.... ss: In the .... Court

.... of .... at ....

I, ...
(Full true name, without abbreviation, and any other name which has been used, must appear here.)

now residing at ....
(Number and street) (City or town) (County) (State)

occupation ...., aged .... years, do declare on oath that my personal description is:

Sex ...., color ...., complexion ...., color of eyes ....

color of hair ...., height .... feet .... inches; weight .... pounds; visible distinctive marks

race ....; nationality ....

I was born in ...., on ....
(City or town) (Country) (Month) (Day) (Year)

I am .... married. The name of my wife or husband is ....

we were married on ...., at ....; she or he was
(Month) (Day) (Year) (City or town) (State or country)

born at ...., on ...., entered the United States
(City or town) (State or country) (Month) (Day) (Year)

at ...., on ...., for permanent residence therein, and now
(City or town) (State) (Month) (Day) (Year)

resides at .... I have .... children, and the name, date and place of birth,
(City or town) (State or country)

and place of residence of each of said children are as follows: ....

....

....

I have .... heretofore made a declaration of intention: Number ...., on ....
(Date)

at ....
(City or town) (State) (Name of court)

my last foreign residence was ....
(City or town) (Country)

I emigrated to the United States of America from ....
(City or town) (Country)

my lawful entry for permanent residence in the United States was at ....
(City or town) (State)

under the name of ...., on ....
(Month) (Day) (Year)

on the vessel ....
(If other than by vessel, state manner of arrival)

I will, before being admitted to citizenship, renounce forever all allegiance and fidelity to any foreign prince, potentate, state, or sovereignty, and particularly, by name, to the prince, potentate, state, or sovereignty of which I may be at the time of admission a citizen or subject; I am not an anarchist; I am not a polygamist nor a believer in the practice of polygamy; and it is my intention in good faith to become a citizen of the United States of America and to reside permanently therein; and I certify that the photograph affixed to the duplicate and triplicate hereof is a likeness of me: SO HELP ME GOD.

[DO NOT ATTACH PHOTOGRAPH TO THIS COPY OF DECLARATION]

....
(Original signature of declarant without abbreviation, also alias, if used)

Subscribed and sworn to before me in the office of the Clerk of said Court, at ...., this .... day of .... anno Domini 19........ Certification No. .... from the Commissioner of Naturalization showing the lawful entry of the declarant for permanent residence on the date stated above, has been received by me. The photograph affixed to the duplicate and triplicate hereof is a likeness of the declarant.

[SEAL]

Form 2202—L-A.
U. S. DEPARTMENT OF LABOR
NATURALIZATION SERVICE

....
Clerk of the .... Court.

By ...., Deputy Clerk.

14—2623

Repository ....; Film number ....; Volume and page ....;
Date researched ....; Copy of original made ....?; Researcher's Notes:

52 • *Documents of Our Ancestors*

Declaration of Intention, Form N-315: January 13, 1941–(voluntary after December 24, 1952)

Form N-315
UNITED STATES DEPARTMENT OF JUSTICE
IMMIGRATION AND NATURALIZATION SERVICE
(Rev. 2-3-53)

Form approved.
Budget Bureau No. 43-R076.4.

ORIGINAL
(To be retained by Clerk of Court)

UNITED STATES OF AMERICA

No. ....

DECLARATION OF INTENTION

.... } ss: In the .... Court
.... of .... at ....

(1) My full, true, and correct name is ....
(Full, true name, without abbreviation, and any other name which has been used, must appear here) (2) My present place of residence is ....
(Number and street) (City or town) (County) (State)

(3) I am .... years old. (4) I was born ....
(Month) (Day) (Year)

in ....
(City or town) (County, district, province, or State) (Country) (5) My personal description is as follows: Sex ...., complexion ...., color of eyes ...., color of hair ...., height .... feet .... inches, weight .... pounds, visible distinctive marks ...., country of which I am a citizen, subject, or national ...., (6) I am .... married; the name of of my wife or husband is ....; (7) My lawful admission for permanent residence in the United States was ....
(City or town) (State)
under the name of .... on ....
(Month) (Day) (Year)
on the ....
(Name of vessel or other means of conveyance) and I am now residing in the United States pursuant to such admission. (8) It is my intention in good faith to become a citizen of the United States. (9) I certify that the photograph affixed to the duplicate and triplicate hereof is a likeness of me and was signed by me.

I do swear (affirm) that the statements I have made and the intentions I have expressed in this declaration of intention subscribed by me are true to the best of my knowledge and belief: SO HELP ME GOD.

....
(Original and true signature of declarant without abbreviation, also other name if used)

Subscribed and sworn to (affirmed) before me in the form of oath shown above in the office of the Clerk of said Court, at ...., this .... anno Domini 19........ I hereby certify that authorization for the issuance of this declaration has been received by me from the Immigration and Naturalization Service, and that the photograph affixed to the duplicate and triplicate hereof is a likeness of the declarant.

....
Clerk of the ....
(Court)

[SEAL]

(Do not attach photograph to this copy of declaration)

By ....
Deputy Clerk.

U. S. GOVERNMENT PRINTING OFFICE 16—67747-2

Repository ....; Film number ....; Volume and page ....;
Date researched ....; Copy of original made ....?; Researcher's Notes:

A Selection of Reproducible Genealogy Forms and Tips for Using Them • 53

Old Law (pre-1906) Petition for Naturalization

UNITED STATES OF AMERICA.

STATE OF _____ } ss.

COUNTY OF _____

Be it Known, That on the _____ day of _____ 18*5__, at the _____ Term, 18*5__, of the _____ Circuit Court, personally appeared in open Court _____

_____

a native of _____ and shows to the Court by a certificate under seal that on the _____ day of _____ 18__ he reported himself for **NATURALIZATION**, and declared his intentions preparatory to being admitted **A CITIZEN OF THE UNITED STATES**, before the _____ _____ agreeably to the act of Congress in such case made and provided. And proves by the examination of two competent witnesses, his residence in the United States more than five years, and in the State of _____ one year, his attachment to the principles of the Constitution of the United States, and favorable disposition to the good order and happiness of the same, and likewise his behavior as a man of good moral character.

Thereupon said _____ is duly sworn in open Court, and makes oath that he will **SUPPORT THE CONSTITUTION OF THE UNITED STATES**, and that he does absolutely and entirely **RENOUNCE AND ABJURE ALL ALLEGIANCE AND FIDELITY TO EVERY FOREIGN PRINCE, POTENTATE, STATE, OR SOVEREIGNTY WHATEVER:** and particularly to _____

_____

In witness whereof, I hereunto set my name _____ this _____ day of _____ A. D., 18__

_____ *Clerk.*

Repository _____; Film number _____; Volume and page _____;
Date researched _____; Copy of original made _____?; Researcher's Notes:

Petition for Naturalization, Form 2204: 1913 – June 30, 1929

Form 2204
U. S. DEPARTMENT OF LABOR
NATURALIZATION SERVICE

ORIGINAL

No. _____

UNITED STATES OF AMERICA
PETITION FOR NATURALIZATION

To the Honorable the _____ Court of _____ at _____

The petition of _____ hereby filed, respectfully showeth:

First. My place of residence is _____ (give number, street, city or town, and State).

Second. My occupation is _____

Third. I was born on the _____ day of _____, anno Domini 1_____ at _____

Fourth. I emigrated to the United States from _____ on or about the _____ day of _____, anno Domini 1_____, and arrived in the United States, at the port of _____, on the _____ day of _____, anno Domini 1_____, on the vessel _____ (If the alien arrived otherwise than by vessel, the character of conveyance or name of transportation company should be given.)

Fifth. I declared my intention to become a citizen of the United States on the _____ day of _____, anno Domini 1_____, at _____, in the _____ Court of _____

Sixth. I am _____ married. My {wife's/husband's} name is _____, she/he was born in _____ on the _____ day of _____, anno Domini 1_____, and now resides at _____ (give number, street, city or town, and State).

I have _____ children, and the name, date, and place of birth, and place of residence of each of said children is as follows:

_____
_____
_____
_____
_____
_____

Seventh. I am not a disbeliever in or opposed to organized government or a member of or affiliated with any organization or body of persons teaching disbelief in or opposed to organized government. I am not a polygamist nor a believer in the practice of polygamy. I am attached to the principles of the Constitution of the United States, and it is my intention to become a citizen of the United States and to renounce absolutely and forever all allegiance and fidelity to any foreign prince, potentate, state, or sovereignty, and particularly to _____ of whom at this time I am a subject, and it is my intention to reside permanently in the United States.

Eighth. I am able to speak the English language.

Ninth. I have resided continuously in the United States of America for the term of five years at least immediately preceding the date of this petition, to wit, since the _____ day of _____, anno Domini 1_____, and in the State of _____ continuously next preceding the date of this petition, since the _____ day of _____, anno Domini 1_____, being a residence within this State of at least one year next preceding the date of this petition.

Tenth. I have not heretofore made petition for citizenship to any court. (I made petition for citizenship to the _____ Court of _____ at _____ on the _____ day of _____, anno Domini 1_____, and the said petition was denied by the said Court for the following reasons and causes, to wit: _____ and the cause of such denial has since been cured or removed.)

Attached hereto and made a part of this petition are my declaration of intention to become a citizen of the United States and the certificate from the Department of Labor, together with my affidavit and the affidavits of the two verifying witnesses thereto, required by law. Wherefore your petitioner prays that he may be admitted a citizen of the United States of America.

_____ (Complete and true signature of petitioner.)

Declaration of Intention No. _____ and Certificate of Arrival from Department of Labor filed this _____ day of _____, 19_____.

NOTE TO CLERK OF COURT.—If petitioner arrived in the United States on or before June 29, 1906, strike out the words reading "and Certificate of Arrival from Department of Labor."

AFFIDAVITS OF PETITIONER AND WITNESSES

_____ } ss:

The aforesaid petitioner being duly sworn, deposes and says that he is the petitioner in the above-entitled proceedings; that he has read the foregoing petition and knows the contents thereof; that the said petition is signed with his full, true name; that the same is true of his own knowledge, except as to matters therein stated to be alleged upon information and belief, and that as to those matters he believes it to be true.

_____ (Complete and true signature of petitioner.)

_____, occupation _____, residing at _____

and _____, occupation _____, residing at _____

each being severally, duly, and respectively sworn, deposes and says that he is a citizen of the United States of America; that he has personally known _____, the petitioner above mentioned, to have resided in the United States continuously immediately preceding the date of filing his petition, since the _____ day of _____, anno Domini 1_____; and in the State in which the above-entitled petition is made continuously since the _____ day of _____, anno Domini 1_____; and that he has personal knowledge that the said petitioner is a person of good moral character, attached to the principles of the Constitution of the United States, and that the petitioner is in every way qualified, in his opinion, to be admitted a citizen of the United States.

_____ (Signature of witness.)

_____ (Signature of witness.)

Subscribed and sworn to before me by the above-named petitioner and witnesses in the office of the Clerk of said Court this _____ day of _____, anno Domini 19_____.

[SEAL]

_____, Clerk.

By _____, Deputy Clerk.

[OVER]

Form 2204, reverse side

IN THE MATTER OF THE PETITION OF

_____

Filed _____, 19___

TO BE ADMITTED A CITIZEN OF THE UNITED STATES OF AMERICA.

OATH OF ALLEGIANCE

I hereby declare, on oath, that I absolutely and entirely renounce and abjure all allegiance and fidelity to any foreign prince, potentate, state, or sovereignty, and particularly to _____ the _____ of _____ of whom I have heretofore been a subject; that I will support and defend the Constitution and laws of the United States of America against all enemies, foreign and domestic; and that I will bear true faith and allegiance to the same.

_____

Subscribed and sworn to before me, in open Court, this _____ day of _____, A. D. 19____

_____, Clerk.

NOTE—In renunciation of title of nobility, add the following to the oath of allegiance before it is executed: "I further renounce the title of (give title), an order of nobility, which I have heretofore held."

ORDER OF COURT ADMITTING PETITIONER

Upon consideration of the petition of _____, and affidavits in support thereof, and further testimony taken in open Court, it is ordered that the said petitioner, who has taken the oath required by law, be, and hereby is, admitted to become a citizen of the United States of America, this _____ day of _____, A. D. 19____

(It is further ordered, upon consideration of the petition of the said _____, that his name be, and hereby is, changed to _____, under authority of the provisions of section 6 of the act approved June 29, 1906 (34 Stat. L., pt. 1, p. 596), as amended by the act approved March 4, 1913, entitled "An act to create a Department of Labor.")

By the Court:

_____, Judge.

ORDER OF COURT DENYING PETITION

Upon consideration of the petition of _____ and the motion of _____ for the United States in open Court this _____ day of _____, 19____, it appearing that _____

_____

_____

THE SAID PETITION IS HEREBY DENIED.

_____, Judge.

MEMORANDUM OF CONTINUANCES

REASONS FOR CONTINUANCE

Continued from _____, 19____ _____
  to _____, 19____
Continued from _____, 19____ _____
  to _____, 19____

NAMES OF SUBSTITUTED WITNESSES

_____, occupation _____, residing at _____
_____, occupation _____, residing at _____

Certificate of Naturalization, No. _____, issued on the _____ day of _____, A. D. 19____

[INSERT ON FOLLOWING LINES MARRIAGES AND BIRTHS OCCURRING AFTER PETITIONING AND BEFORE NATURALIZATION.]

_____

_____

Repository _____; Film number _____; Volume and page _____;
Date researched _____; Copy of original made _____?; Researcher's Notes:

---

56 • *Documents of Our Ancestors*

Petition for Naturalization, Form 2204 L-A: July 1, 1929 – January 13, 1941

ORIGINAL
(To be retained by clerk)

UNITED STATES OF AMERICA
PETITION FOR NATURALIZATION

No. _____

To the Honorable the _____ Court of _____ at _____

The petition of _____, hereby filed, respectfully shows:

(1) My place of residence is _____ (2) My occupation is _____

(3) I was born in _____ on _____ My race is _____

(4) I declared my intention to become a citizen of the United States on _____ in the Court of _____ at _____

(5) I am _____ married. The name of my wife or husband is _____ we were married on _____ at _____; he was born at _____ on _____; entered the United States at _____ on _____ for permanent residence therein, and now resides at _____; was _____ naturalized on _____ at _____ certificate No. _____ I have _____ children, and the name, date, and place of birth, and place of residence of each of said children are as follows: _____

_____

(6) My last foreign residence was _____. I emigrated to the United States of America from _____. My lawful entry for permanent residence in the United States was at _____, under the name of _____ on _____, on the vessel _____ as shown by the certificate of my arrival attached hereto.

(7) I am not a disbeliever in or opposed to organized government or a member of or affiliated with any organization or body of persons teaching disbelief in or opposed to organized government. I am not a polygamist nor a believer in the practice of polygamy. I am attached to the principles of the Constitution of the United States and well disposed to the good order and happiness of the United States. It is my intention to become a citizen of the United States and to renounce absolutely and forever all allegiance and fidelity to any foreign prince, potentate, state, or sovereignty, of whom (which) at this time I am a subject (or citizen), and it is my intention to reside permanently in the United States. (8) I am able to speak the English language. (9) I have resided continuously in the United States of America for the term of 5 years at least immediately preceding the date of this petition, to wit, since _____ and in the County of _____ this State, continuously next preceding the date of this petition, since _____, being a residence within said county of at least 6 months next preceding the date of this petition.

(10) I have _____ heretofore made petition for naturalization: No. _____ on _____ at _____ and such petition was denied by that Court for the following reasons and causes, to wit: _____ and the cause of such denial has since been cured or removed.

Attached hereto and made a part of this, my petition for naturalization, are my declaration of intention to become a citizen of the United States, certificate from the Department of Labor of my said arrival, and the affidavits of the two verifying witnesses required by law.

Wherefore, I, your petitioner, pray that I may be admitted a citizen of the United States of America, and that my name be changed to _____

I, _____, do swear (affirm) that I know the contents of this petition for naturalization subscribed by me, that the same are true to the best of my own knowledge, except as to matters therein stated to be alleged upon information and belief, and as to those matters I believe them to be true, and that this petition was signed by me with my full, true name: SO HELP ME GOD.

_____
(Complete and true signature of petitioner)

AFFIDAVITS OF WITNESSES

_____, occupation _____, residing at _____ and _____, occupation _____, residing at _____, each being severally, duly, and respectively sworn, deposes and says: I am a citizen of the United States of America; I have personally known and have been acquainted in the United States with _____, the petitioner above mentioned, since _____ and that to my personal knowledge the petitioner has resided in the United States continuously preceding the date of filing this petition, of which this affidavit is a part, to wit, since the date last mentioned and at _____ in the County of _____ this State, in which the above-entitled petition is made, continuously since _____ and that I have personal knowledge that the petitioner is and during all such periods has been a person of good moral character, attached to the principles of the Constitution of the United States, and well disposed to the good order and happiness of the United States, and in my opinion the petitioner is in every way qualified to be admitted a citizen of the United States.

I do swear (affirm) that the statements of fact I have made in this affidavit of this petition for naturalization subscribed by me are true to the best of my knowledge and belief.

_____   _____
(Signature of witness)   (Signature of witness)

Subscribed and sworn to before me by the above-named petitioner and witnesses in the respective forms of oath shown above in the office of Clerk of said Court at _____ this _____ day of _____ Anno Domini 19____. I hereby certify that Certificate of Arrival No. _____ from the Department of Labor, showing the lawful entry for permanent residence of the petitioner above named, together with Declaration of Intention No. _____ of such petitioner, has been by me filed with, attached to, and made a part of this petition on this date.

_____ [SEAL]
Clerk

By _____
Deputy

FORM 2204—L-A
U. S. DEPARTMENT OF LABOR
IMMIGRATION AND NATURALIZATION SERVICE

Repository _____; Film number _____; Volume and page _____;
Date researched _____; Copy of original made _____?; Researcher's Notes:

A Selection of Reproducible Genealogy Forms and Tips for Using Them • 57

Petition for Naturalization, Form N-405: January 1, 1941 –

ORIGINAL
(To be retained by Clerk of Court)

UNITED STATES OF AMERICA

No. _____

PETITION FOR NATURALIZATION
[Under General Provisions of the Nationality Act of 1940 (Public, No. 853, 76th Cong.)]

To the Honorable the _____ Court of _____ at _____
This petition for naturalization, hereby made and filed, respectively shows:

(1) My full, true, and correct name is _____
(Full, true name, without abbreviation, and any other name which has been used, must appear here)
(2) My present place of residence is _____ (3) My occupation is _____
(Number and street) (City or town) (County) (State)
(4) I am _____ years old. (5) I was born on _____, in _____
(Month) (Day) (Year) (City or town) (County, district, province, or state) (Country)
(6) My personal description is as follows: Sex _____, color _____, complexion _____, color of eyes _____, color of hair _____,
height _____ feet _____ inches, weight _____ pounds, visible distinctive marks _____, race _____,
present nationality _____ (7) I am _____ married; the name of my wife or husband is _____
we were married on _____ at _____
(Month) (Day) (Year) (City or town) (State or country)
he or she was born at _____, on _____
(City or town) (County, district, province, or state) (Country) (Month) (Day) (Year)
and entered the United States at _____ on _____ for permanent residence in the United States
(City or town) (State) (Month) (Day) (Year)
and now resides at _____ and was naturalized on _____
(Number and street) (City or town) (County and State) (Month) (Day) (Year)
at _____ certificate No. _____; or became a citizen by _____
(City or town) (State)
(8) I have _____ children; and the name, sex, date and place of birth, and present place of residence of each of said children who is living, are as follows:

_____
_____
_____
_____

(9) My last place of foreign residence was _____ (10) I emigrated to the United States from
(City or town) (County, district, province, or state) (Country)
_____ (11) My lawful entry for permanent residence in the United States was
(City or town) (Country)
at _____ under the name of _____
(City or town) (State)
on _____ on the _____
(Month) (Day) (Year) (Name of vessel or other means of conveyance)
as shown by the certificate of my arrival attached to this petition.
(12) Since my lawful entry for permanent residence I have _____ been absent from the United States, for a period or periods of 6 months or longer, as follows:

DEPARTED FROM THE UNITED STATES			RETURNED TO THE UNITED STATES		
Port	Date (Month, day, year)	Vessel or other means of Conveyance	Port	Date (Month, day, year)	Vessel or other means of Conveyance

(13) I declared my intention to become a citizen of the United States on _____ in the _____
(Month) (Day) (Year) (Name of court)
Court of _____ at _____ (14) It is my intention in good faith to become a
(City or town) (State)
citizen of the United States and to renounce absolutely and forever all allegiance and fidelity to any foreign prince, potentate, State, or sovereignty of whom or which at this time I am a subject or citizen, and it is my intention to reside permanently in the United States. (15) I am not, and have not been for the period of at least 10 years immediately preceding the date of this petition, an anarchist; nor a believer in the unlawful damage, injury, or destruction of property, or sabotage; nor a disbeliever in or opposed to organized government; nor a member of or affiliated with any organization or body of persons teaching disbelief in or opposition to organized government. (16) I am able to speak the English language (unless physically unable to do so). (17) I am, and have been during all of the periods required by law, attached to the principles of the Constitution of the United States and well disposed to the good order and happiness of the United States. (18) I have resided continuously in the United States of America for the term of 5 years at least immediately preceding the date of this petition, to wit, since _____
(Month) (Day) (Year)
and continuously in the State in which this petition is made for the term of 6 months at least immediately preceding the date of this petition, to wit, since
_____ (19) I have _____ heretofore made petition for naturalization: No. _____
(Month) (Day) (Year)
on _____ at _____ in the _____
(Month) (Day) (Year) (City or town) (County) (State) (Name of court)
Court, and such petition was dismissed or denied by that Court for the following reasons and causes, to wit: _____
_____ and the cause of such dismissal or denial has since been cured or removed.
(20) Attached hereto and made a part of this, my petition for naturalization, are my declaration of intention to become a citizen of the United States (if such declaration of intention be required by the naturalization law), a certificate of arrival from the Immigration and Naturalization Service of my said lawful entry into the United States for permanent residence (if such certificate of arrival be required by the naturalization law), and the affidavits of at least two verifying witnesses required by law.
(21) Wherefore, I, your petitioner for naturalization, pray that I may be admitted a citizen of the United States of America, and that my name be changed to _____
(22) I, aforesaid petitioner, do swear (affirm) that I know the contents of this petition for naturalization subscribed by me, that the same are true to the best of my own knowledge, except as to matters therein stated to be alleged upon information and belief, and that as to those matters I believe them to be true, and that this petition is signed by me with my full, true name: SO HELP ME GOD.

_____
(Full, true, and correct signature of petitioner, without abbreviation)

Form N-405
U. S. DEPARTMENT OF JUSTICE
IMMIGRATION AND NATURALIZATION SERVICE
(Edition of 1-10-41)

Repository _____; Film number _____; Volume and page _____;
Date researched _____; Copy of original made _____?; Researcher's Notes:

United States of America
Immigration and Naturalization Service

Alien Registration Form

1. ☆(a) My name is _____
         (FIRST NAME)   (MIDDLE NAME)   (LAST NAME)
   ☆(b) I entered the United States under the name of _____
   ☆(c) I have also been known by the following names _____
        (include maiden name if a married woman,
        professional names, nicknames, and aliases): _____
2. ☆(a) I live at _____
                (STREET ADDRESS OR RURAL ROUTE)   (CITY)   (COUNTY)   (STATE)
   ☆(b) My post-office address is _____
                                  (POST OFFICE)   (STATE)
3. ☆(a) I was born on _____
                      (MONTH)   (DAY)   (YEAR)
   ☆(b) I was born in (or near) _____
                                (CITY)   (PROVINCE)   (COUNTRY)
4. ☆   I am a citizen or subject of _____
                                    (COUNTRY)

5. ☆(a) I am a (*check one*):   ☆(b) My marital status is (*check one*):
       Male...☐¹   Female...☐²   Single...☐¹   Married..,☐²   Widowed...☐³   Divorced...☐⁴
   ☆(c) My race is (*check one*): White...☐¹   Negro...☐²   Japanese...☐³   Chinese...☐⁴   Other _____
6. I am _____ feet _____ inches in height, weigh _____ pounds, have _____ hair and _____ eyes.
                                                                       (COLOR)   (COLOR)
7. ☆(a) I last arrived in the United States at _____
                                               (PORT OR PLACE OF ENTRY)
   ☆(b) I came in by _____
        (NAME OF VESSEL, STEAMSHIP COMPANY, OR OTHER MEANS OF TRANSPORTATION)

   ☆(c) I came as a (*check one*) Passenger...☐¹   Crew member...☐²   Stowaway...☐³   Other _____
   ☆(d) I entered the United States as a (*check one*): Permanent resident...☐¹   Visitor...☐²   Student...☐³
        Treaty merchant...☐⁴   Seaman...☐⁵   Official of a foreign government...☐⁶   Employee of a
        foreign government official...☐⁷   Other _____
   ☆(e) I first arrived in the United States on _____
                                                (MONTH)   (DAY)   (YEAR)
8. ☆(a) I have lived in the United States a total of _____ years
   ☆(b) I expect to remain in the United States _____
                                                (PERMANENTLY, OR DURATION OF EXPECTED STAY)

9. (a) My usual occupation is _____ (b) My present occupation is _____
   ☆(c) My employer (or registering parent or guardian) is _____
                                                           (NAME)
        whose address is _____
                         (STREET ADDRESS OR RURAL ROUTE)   (CITY)   (STATE)
        and whose business is _____

All items must be answered by persons 14 years of age or older. For children under 14 years of age, only the items marked with a star (☆) must be answered by the parent or guardian. All answers must be accurate and complete.

A Selection of Reproducible Genealogy Forms and Tips for Using Them

10. I am, or have been within the past 3 years, or intend to be engaged in the following activities:

In addition to other information, list memberships or activities in clubs, organizations, or societies _____
_____
_____
_____

11. My military or naval service has been _____
                                                                          (COUNTRY)
_____ From _____ to _____
            (BRANCH OF SERVICE)   (DATE)   (DATE)

12. ☆I _____ applied for citizenship papers in the United States. Date of application _____
     (HAVE. HAVE NOT)

13. ☆I have the following specified relatives living in the United States:
    Parent(s) _____ Husband or wife _____ Children _____
    (NONE. OR ONE. OR BOTH)   (YES OR NO)   (NUMBER)

14. I _____ been arrested or indicted for, or convicted of any offense (or offenses). These offenses are:
   (HAVE. HAVE NOT)
_____ _____ _____ _____ _____
_____ _____

15. Within the past 5 years I _____ been affiliated with or active in (a member of, official of, a
                            (HAVE. HAVE NOT)
worker for) organizations, devoted in whole or in part to
influencing or furthering the political activities, public
relations, or public policy of a foreign government. _____

AFFIDAVIT FOR PERSONS 14 YEARS OF AGE AND OLDER

Right Index Finger

    I have read or have had read to me the above statements, and do hereby swear (or affirm) that these statements are true and complete to the best of my knowledge and belief.

    Subscribed and sworn to (or affirmed) before me at the place and on the date here designated by the official post-office stamp below.

_____   _____
(SIGNATURE OF REGISTRANT)   (REGISTERING OFFICIAL)

AFFIDAVIT FOR PARENT OR GUARDIAN ONLY

I am the _____
(PARENT OF, OR GUARDIAN OF, OR PERSON RESPONSIBLE FOR)
the above-named alien, who is _____
                       (UNDER 14 YEARS OF AGE, OR INSANE)
and have made the above allegations for him
(or her). I have read or have had the same read
to me, and do hereby swear (or affirm) that
they are true and complete to the best of my
knowledge, information, and belief.

PRINT NAME, ADDRESS,
AND BUSINESS OF PERSON
SIGNING THIS AFFIDAVIT IN
9(C), ABOVE.

    Subscribed and sworn to
(or affirmed) before me at the
place and on the date here
designated by the official
post-office stamp at the right.

_____   _____
(SIGNATURE OF PARENT OF, OR GUARDIAN OF, OR PERSON   (REGISTERING OFFICIAL)
RESPONSIBLE FOR THE ALIEN)

Repository _____ ; Film number _____ ; Volume and page _____ ; Date researched _____ ;
Copy of original made _____ ?; Researcher's Notes: _____

Veterans Records

Forms Provided

A. *National Archives Order for Copies of Veterans Records (NATF Form 80 (rev. 10-93)*
(Note: This is a multi-part form. An original must be requested from: National Archives Trust Fund, P.O. Box 100221, Atlanta, GA 30384-0221.)

The form and its instructions provides complete information about what is available and how to obtain the records.

An abstract of these records is not provided here since the photocopies of the records almost always are provided by mail from the source and are not in a standardized format.

Additional Help

National Archives Trust Fund Board, *Military Service Records: A Select Catalog of National Archives Microfilm Publications,* 1985. (Available on the WWW at <http://www.nara.gov>.

Petree, David L., and Thomas G. Hudson, "Selective Service, Military Personnel, and Federal Civilian Employee Records," *Dorot,* vol. 14, no. 4, Summer 1993.

NATIONAL ARCHIVES ORDER FOR COPIES OF VETERANS RECORDS

Dear Researcher,

Before completing the form, please read both sides of this page for ordering instructions and general information about the types of records that can be ordered with this form. Mail order photocopying service by using this form is available **ONLY** from *General Reference Branch (NNRG-P), National Archives and Records Administration, 7th and Pennsylvania Avenue NW., Washington, DC 20408.* For more information, please write to us at the address above.

IMPORTANT INFORMATION ABOUT YOUR ORDER

The success of our search depends on the completeness and accuracy of the information you provide in blocks 3-18 on this form. Please note that each NATF Form 80 is handled separately. When you send more than one form at a time, you may not receive all of your replies at the same time.

Military service records rarely contain family information. Pension application files generally are most useful to those who are doing genealogical research and contain the most complete information regarding a man's military career. We suggest that you first request copies of a man's pension file. You should request copies of a bounty-land warrant file or a military record only when no pension file exists. If the veteran's service was during the Revolutionary War, bounty-land warrant applications have been consolidated with pension application papers. You can obtain both files by requesting the pension file only.

We will copy complete compiled military service and bounty-land application files. When we are unable to provide copies of all pension documents because of the size of a pension application file, we will send copies of the documents we think will be most useful to you for genealogical purposes. Many of the documents in these files are repetitive or administrative in nature. You may order copies of all remaining documents in a file by making a specific request. We will notify you of the cost of the additional copies.

Do NOT use this form to request photocopies of records relating to service in World War I or II, or subsequent service. Write to: *National Personnel Records Center (Military Records), NARA, 9700 Page Boulevard, St. Louis, MO 63132.*

INSTRUCTIONS FOR COMPLETING THIS FORM

Use a separate NATF Form 80 for each file that you request. Remove this instruction sheet. You must complete blocks 3-7 or we cannot search for the file. Print your name (last, first, middle) and address in the block provided at the bottom of the form, which is your mailing label. The information must be legible on all copies. Keep the PINK copy of the form for your records. Mail the remaining three pages of the form to: *General Reference Branch (NNRG-P), National Archives and Records Administration, 7th and Pennsylvania Avenue NW., Washington, DC 20408.* **DO NOT SEND PAYMENT WITH THIS FORM.** When we search your order, we will make photocopies of records that relate to your request. For credit card orders, we will mail the copies immediately. For other types of orders, we will invoice you for the cost of these copies and hold them until we receive your payment.

SEE THE REVERSE OF THIS PAGE FOR DESCRIPTIONS OF THE TYPES OF RECORDS THAT CAN BE ORDERED WITH THIS FORM.

TYPES OF RECORDS THAT CAN BE ORDERED WITH THIS FORM

PENSION APPLICATION FILES

Pension application files, based on Federal (not State) service before World War I, usually include an official statement of the veteran's military service, as well as information of a personal nature. Pensions based on military service for the Confederate States of America were authorized by some Southern States but not by the Federal Government until 1959. Inquiries about State pensions should be addressed to the State archives or equivalent agency at the capital of the veteran's State of residence after the war.

BOUNTY-LAND WARRANT APPLICATION FILES

Bounty-land warrant application files are based on Federal (not State) service before 1856. Documents in a bounty-land warrant application file are similar to those in a pension application file. In addition, these files usually give the veteran's age and place of residence at the time the application was made.

MILITARY SERVICE RECORDS

Military service records are based on service in the UNITED STATES ARMY (officers who served before June 30, 1917, and enlisted men who served before October 31, 1912); NAVY (officers who served before 1903 and enlisted men who served before 1886); MARINE CORPS (officers who served before 1896 and enlisted men who served before 1905); and CONFEDERATE ARMED FORCES (officers and enlisted men, 1861-65). In addition to persons who served in regular forces raised by the Federal Government, volunteers fought in various wars chiefly in the Federal Government's interest from the Revolutionary War through the Philippine Insurrection, 1775-1902.

Compilations of information concerning most military service performed by individuals in volunteer organizations during the 19th and early 20th centuries are available, but such records were not compiled for Regular Army officers who served before 1863 and for Regular Army enlisted men and Navy and Marine Corps personnel who served during most of the 19th century. Records pertaining to such service are scattered among many files and generally contain few details concerning a man's service. We cannot undertake the research necessary to locate all such documents. If you request a military service record, we will copy the documents that best summarize the veteran's service.

The record of an individual's service in any one organization is entirely separate from his record of service in another organization. We are unable to establish accurately the identity of individuals of the same name who served in different organizations. If you know that an individual served in more than one organization and you desire copies of all of the military service records, submit a separate form for the service record in each organization.

Discharge certificates are not usually included as a part of a compiled military service record. Before 1944, Army regulations allowed the preparation of an original discharge certificate only, which was given to the soldier. Confederate soldiers in service at the time of surrender did not receive discharge certificates. They were given paroles, and these paroles became the property of the soldier.

NATIONAL ARCHIVES
ORDER FOR COPIES OF VETERANS RECORDS
(See Instructions page before completing this form)

DATE RECEIVED IN NNRG

INDICATE BELOW THE TYPE OF FILE DESIRED AND THE METHOD OF PAYMENT PREFERRED.

1. FILE TO BE SEARCHED *(Check one box only)*
- ☐ PENSION
- ☐ BOUNTY-LAND WARRANT APPLICATION *(Service before 1856 only)*
- ☐ MILITARY

2. PAYMENT METHOD *(Check one box only)*

☐ **CREDIT CARD** *(VISA or MasterCard) for IMMEDIATE SHIPMENT of copies*
Account Number: _____ Exp. Date: _____
Signature: _____ Daytime Phone: _____

☐ **BILL ME** *(No Credit Card)*

REQUIRED MINIMUM IDENTIFICATION OF VETERAN – MUST BE COMPLETED OR YOUR ORDER CANNOT BE SERVICED

3. VETERAN *(Give last, first, and middle names)*

4. BRANCH OF SERVICE IN WHICH HE SERVED
☐ ARMY ☐ NAVY ☐ MARINE CORPS

5. STATE FROM WHICH HE SERVED

6. WAR IN WHICH, OR DATES BETWEEN WHICH, HE SERVED

7. IF SERVICE WAS CIVIL WAR,
☐ UNION ☐ CONFEDERATE

PLEASE PROVIDE THE FOLLOWING ADDITIONAL INFORMATION, IF KNOWN

8. UNIT IN WHICH HE SERVED *(Name of regiment or number, company, etc., name of ship)*

9. IF SERVICE WAS ARMY, ARM IN WHICH HE SERVED
☐ INFANTRY ☐ CAVALRY ☐ ARTILLERY

If other, specify:

Rank: ☐ OFFICER ☐ ENLISTED

10. KIND OF SERVICE
☐ VOLUNTEERS ☐ REGULARS

11. PENSION/BOUNTY-LAND FILE NO.

12. IF VETERAN LIVED IN A HOME FOR SOLDIERS, GIVE LOCATION *(City and State)*

13. PLACE(S) VETERAN LIVED AFTER SERVICE

14. DATE OF BIRTH

15. PLACE OF BIRTH *(City, County, State, etc.)*

18. NAME OF WIDOW OR OTHER CLAIMANT

16. DATE OF DEATH

17. PLACE OF DEATH *(City, County, State, etc.)*

NATIONAL ARCHIVES TRUST FUND BOARD   NATF Form 80 (rev. 10-93)

DO NOT WRITE BELOW – SPACE IS FOR OUR REPLY TO YOU

☐ **NO**—We were unable to locate the file you requested above. No payment is required.

DATE SEARCHED | SEARCHER

☐ **REQUIRED MINIMUM IDENTIFICATION OF VETERAN WAS NOT PROVIDED.** Please complete blocks 3 (give full name), 4, 5, 6, and 7 and resubmit your order.

☐ **A SEARCH WAS MADE BUT THE FILE YOU REQUESTED ABOVE WAS NOT FOUND.** When we do not find a record for a veteran, this does not mean that he did not serve. You may be able to obtain information about him from the archives of the State from which he served.

☐ See attached forms, leaflets, or information sheets.

☐ **YES**—We located the file you requested above. We have made copies from the file for you. The cost for these copies is $10.

DATE SEARCHED | SEARCHER

FILE DESIGNATION

Make your check or money order payable to NATIONAL ARCHIVES TRUST FUND. Do not send cash. Return this form and your payment in the enclosed envelope to:

NATIONAL ARCHIVES TRUST FUND
P.O. BOX 100221
ATLANTA, GA 30384-0221

PLEASE NOTE: We will hold these copies awaiting receipt of payment for only 45 days from the date completed, which is stamped below. After that time, you must submit another form to obtain photocopies of the file.

THIS IS YOUR MAILING LABEL. PRESS FIRMLY.

NAME (Last, First, MI)
STREET
CITY STATE   ZIP CODE

(A893774)

INVOICE/REPLY COPY – DO NOT DETACH

Social Security Records

Forms Provided

    A. *Social Security Death Index abstract form*
    B. *Application for Social Security Account Number* (Form SS-5)

What Records Are Available

    The Social Security Death Index (SSDI) covers over 50 million names of holders of social security cards who died through the present date. The index includes almost all deaths reported to the Social Security Administration (SSA) after 1962, plus a significant number of those who died earlier. The Index information is useful in itself, but is most useful in accessing the original Application for Social Security Account Number, or form SS-5. Since no privacy protection is afforded deceased people, copies of the SS-5 are readily available from the Social Security Administration by providing the social security number given in the index. SS-5 forms can serve as a surrogate birth certificate by indicating date and place of birth (unfortunately, usually only the country if foreign born), parents' names, as well as address at time of application, and place of employment.

Where to Find Them

    This index is available at LDS Family History Centers on compact disk. Up-to-date CD-ROM versions also can be purchased commercially, usually for about $35–40.

What You Need Before You Search

    In searching a database of this size, there is a high probability of finding several people with the same name. The more you know before you begin a search, the more likely you will be successful. The most important information is: surname, first name, birth date (within a year or so), and state where social security application was filed.

Tips

- Columns are provided on the abstract form to copy up to four possible "finds," since the likelihood of finding more than one possibility is quite high. The first column can be used to indicate the information you may have available before beginning the search.
- The index information as shown on the form is for copying information directly from the computer screen. Alternatively, the selected records can be printed one record at a time or in groups of records, or copied to your computer disk for printing at home using a word processing program,
- In searching for women, look under their most recent married name.
- The address to write for the SS-5 is: Freedom of Information Officer, Social Security Administration, 4H8 Annex Building, 6401 Security Boulevard, Baltimore, MD 21235. Request a photocopy of the original, not a computer printout. The fee is $7.00 each, or $16.50 if no social security number is provided. No form is required. Just send a letter giving name, social security number, and date of death. It usually takes 6–8 weeks to reply.
- The Social Security Administration has files on everyone registered but will provide information only on deceased persons. While the SSA will not provide addresses, it will forward a letter to the addressee under very strict conditions (review the InfoFile, below, then request form SSA-L963).
- Although an abstract of Form SS-5 is provided here, it will rarely be necessary to use since the SSA will provide a microfilm of the original.

A Selection of Reproducible Genealogy Forms and Tips for Using Them • 65

Additional Help

Bodensteiner, Carrie E., "The Social Security Death Index," <http://www.mtjeff.com/~bodenst/ssdi.html>, April 1996.

JewishGen InfoFile, "Social Security Administration FAQ, <http://www.jewishgen.org>, May 1995.

Kolinsky, Elaine Bunny, "The Social Security Death Index," *Avotaynu,* vol., VIII, no. 1, Spring 1993 p. 12.

"Social Security Death Index is New Genealogical Resource," *Avotaynu,* vol. VII, no. 1, Spring 1992 (no author).

U.S. Social Security Death Index, Series FS, No. 3, folder published by the Church of Jesus Christ of Latter Day Saints, November 1990.

Social Security Death Index
Individual Record

Page_____

NAME (Last)_____ (First)_____ (MI)_____

	Record 1	Record 2	Record 3	Record 4
Birth Date	__/__/____	__/__/____	__/__/____	__/__/____
SS No.	___-__-____	___-__-____	___-__-____	___-__-____
State of Issuance	_____	_____	_____	_____
Death Date	__/__/____	__/__/____	__/__/____	__/__/____
Death ZIP	_____	_____	_____	_____
Death Residence State/Locality	_____	_____	_____	_____

Repository _____; Film number _____; Volume and page _____;
Date researched _____; Copy of original made _____?; Researcher's Notes:

A Selection of Reproducible Genealogy Forms and Tips for Using Them

Treasury Department
Internal Revenue Service

U.S. Social Security Act
Application for Account Number
Form SS-5

No. assigned:_____ -- __

1. Print Name _____
              (employee's first name)   (middle name)   (last name)

2. _____ 3. _____
   (street and number)   (post office)

4. _____ 5. _____
  (business name of present employer)   (business address of present employer)

6. _____ 7. _____ 8. _____
 (age at last birthday) (date of birth (month) (day) (year) subject to later verification)) (place of birth)

9. _____ 10. _____
  (father's full name)   (mother's full maiden name)

11. Sex: Male____ Female____ 12. Color: White____ Negro____ Other_____
    (check ✓ which)   (check ✓ which)

13. If Registered with U.S. Employment Service, Give Number of Registration Card _____

14. If You Have Previously Filled Out a Card Like This, Give Number of Registration Card _____

15. _____ 16. _____
  (date signed)   (employee's signature, as usually written)

Repository _____; Film number _____; Volume and page _____;
Date researched _____; Copy of original made _____?; Researcher's Notes:

Part II

New York State Records

Request and recording forms for New York State records are included here because of their potential value for Jewish genealogists, many of whose ancestors lived for a time in the New York area. Similar records are kept by all states. A good source of applications for vital records for all states is: Thomas Jay Kemp, *International Vital Records Handbook*. It can be purchased from the publisher, Genealogical Publishing Co., 1001 N. Calvert Street, Baltimore, MD 21202, or from Avotaynu, P.O. Box 900, Teaneck, NJ 07666. Also of value is: National Center for Health Statistics, *Where to Write for Vital Records* (Washington: Superintendent of Documents, U.S. Government Printing Office, 1990).

New York State Census

Forms Provided

A. *New York State Census recording form*

What Records Are Available

New York State conducted many censuses from the colonial period through 1925. This covers the censuses of 1905, 1915, and 1925.

Where to Find Them

The originals of the censuses for 1905, 1915, and 1925 for the entire state are located at the New York State Archives and Records Administration, Cultural Extension Center, 11th Floor, Empire State Plaza, Albany, NY 12230, (518) 474-8955.

The New York State Library, Cultural Extension Center, 7th Floor, Empire State Plaza, Albany, NY 12230, (518) 474-3092, has the 1915 and 1925 censuses for the entire state, and selected records for other years.

Complete sets of the 1905, 1915, and 1925 censuses are available at the Family History Library in Salt Lake City and through all its Family History Centers.

Copies of the 1905, 1915, and 1925 New York State censuses for New York City are available in the New York Public Library, Microforms Division, Fifth Avenue at 42nd Street, Room 315N, New York, NY 10018, (212) 930-0838.

Copies of the Manhattan portion of the New York State Censuses for 1905, 1915, and 1925 are available at the County Clerk's Office, State Supreme Court, New York City, 60 Centre Street, Room 103B, New York, NY 10007, (212) 374-8587.

What You Need Before You Search

There are no indexes to these censuses. The researcher must have an address for each year being searched in order to locate the Assembly District and Election District in which a particular record may be found. See Tips on ways to find addresses.

Tips

- The 1905, 1915, and 1925 Census are arranged by Assembly District (AD) and Election District (ED) within each county (or New York City borough).
- There is a card index to street names and house numbers for the 1905, 1915, and 1925 census, for the borough of Manhattan, only. (The Bronx is included in the 1905 index since it was part of New York County until 1912.) All three years are listed on a single card. The indexes show the AD and ED of the address for each year. FHL Catalog Information: New York, New York—Census—1905, 1915, 1925.
- These card indexes generally are available (on microfilm) wherever the New York City censuses are found, including the New York Public Library and the Family History Library. Maps for locating the AD and ED for other addresses are available in the Map Division of the New York Public Library for boroughs outside Manhattan. The Family History Library has a copy of maps for the 1925 Census for New York City showing the AD, ED, and block numbers on a set of fiche collectively numbered 6,088,624.
- The Family History Library has published street indexes to the 1915 New York State censuses for the

boroughs of Manhattan and Brooklyn, in both book and microfiche versions. These show, for each address, the AD and ED, and the Family History Library microfilm number where the record is found. FHL Catalog Information: New York, New York (City)—Census—1915.
- The Kings County Clerk's Office, 360 Adams Street, Brooklyn, NY 11201 will do a search for $5.00 for each address in Kings County (Brooklyn).
- The 1905, 1915, and 1925 censuses were identical (see form) except that the 1925 census asked, for naturalized citizens, the year of naturalization and the court—a valuable shortcut for seeking naturalization records.
- Some ways to find addresses are: (1) Check city or borough directories for the particular years or the closest available years. (2) Look for addresses on vital records—births, marriages, and deaths. (3) Extrapolate from the U.S. decennial censuses (although this is not usually successful since people rarely stayed at the same address for five years). (4) Find addresses on naturalization declarations or petitions. (5) Ask older living relatives where they (parents, grandparents) lived in those years. (6) World War I Draft Registrations (1917, 1918) may be useful for the 1915 Census.

Additional Help

Guzik, *Genealogical Resources in the New York Metropolitan Area,* "New York Public Library," pp. 99–105; "Albany," pp. 225–238.

Lainhart, Ann S., *State Census Records* (Baltimore, MD: Genealogical Publishing Co., ca. 1992).

Family History Library, *Research Outline, New York*, Series US-STATES no. 32 (Salt Lake City, UT: The Genealogical Department, Church of Jesus Christ of Latter Day Saints, March 1992).

New York State Census Recording Form

CENSUS YEAR: _____

Enumeration of Inhabitants of Block No. _____, Election District No. _____, Ward No. _____, City or Village _____

Town _____, Assembly District No. _____, County/Borough _____, State of New York.

Name of Institution _____, June 1, 19___, Enumerator _____

Residence Address		Name		Relation to Head	Color	Sex	Age	Nativity	Citizenship		Occupation		Naturalization (1925 only)	
Street	No.	Last,	First						Years	Cit/Al	Trade/Prof	Class	Court	Date
1		2		3	4	5	6	7	8	9	10	11	12	13
1														
2														
3														
4														
5														
6														
7														
8														
9														
10														
11														
12														
13														
14														
15														
16														
17														
18														
19														

Repository _____; Film number _____; Volume and page _____; Date researched _____

Copy of original made _____?; Researcher's notes:

New York State Vital Records

Forms Provided
- A. *Application for Genealogical Services*
- B. *New York State Register of Live Birth*
- C. *New York State Marriage License*
- D. *New York State Certificate of Death*

What Records Are Available

See instructions on the application form.

The New York State Department of Health provides copies of certificates for genealogy use for births, deaths, or marriages that took place in New York State outside of the five boroughs of New York City (except for births occurring in Queens and Richmond counties for the years 1881 through 1897). Records on file date back to 1881 for births and marriages and 1880 for deaths, **except** for records filed in Albany, Buffalo and Yonkers prior to 1914. Applications for records prior to 1914 for these cities must be made directly to the local office.

Requests may be also be made to the local registrar or town clerk of the place where the birth or death occurred or where the marriage certificate was issued. An index to genealogy records is available for searching at the State Archives, located at the Empire State Plaza in Albany. Phone (518) 474-8955 for more information about using this index.

Since these records are most likely to be requested by mail, the original forms usually will be supplied and these replicas will rarely be needed. However, they may be useful to indicate what the record contains, when the original is difficult to read, or when a copy needs to be made to share with other relatives.

Additional Help

Guzik, *Genealogical Resources in the New York Metropolitan Area,* pp. 234–5.

Family History Library, *Research Outline, New York*, Series US-STATES no. 32 (Salt Lake City, UT: The Genealogical Department, Church of Jesus Christ of Latter Day Saints, March 1992).

"Availability of New York State Vital Records,"
<gopher://gopher.health.state.ny.us:70/11/.consumer/.vital>, June 1995.

NEW YORK STATE DEPARTMENT OF HEALTH
Vital Records Section, Genealogy Unit
Corning Tower Building, Empire State Plaza
Albany, New York 12237-0023

General Information and Application for Genealogical Services

VITAL RECORDS COPIES CANNOT BE PROVIDED FOR COMMERCIAL PURPOSES.

1. FEE - $11.00 includes search and uncertified copy or notification of no record.
2. Original records of births and marriages for the entire state begin with 1881, deaths begin with 1880, EXCEPT for records filed in Albany, Buffalo and Yonkers prior to 1914. Applications for these cities should be made directly to the local office.
3. The New York State Department of Health does not have New York City records except for births occurring in Queens and Richmond counties for the years 1881 through 1897.
4. Please read the Administrative Rule Summary on the reverse side of this sheet which specifies years available for genealogical research.

To insure a complete search, provide as much information as possible. Please complete for type of record requested, birth, death OR marriage.

Birth
- Name at Birth _____
- Date of Birth _____
- Place of Birth _____
- Father's Name _____
- Mother's Maiden Name _____

Birth
- Name at Birth _____
- Date of Birth _____
- Place of Birth _____
- Father's Name _____
- Mother's Maiden Name _____

Marriage
- Name of Bride _____
- Name of Groom _____
- Date of Marriage _____
- Place of Marriage and/or License _____

Marriage
- Name of Bride _____
- Name of Groom _____
- Date of Marriage _____
- Place of Marriage and/or License _____

Death
- Name at Death _____
- Date of Death _____ Age at Death _____
- Place of Death _____
- Names of Parents _____
- Name of Spouse _____

Death
- Name at Death _____
- Date of Death _____ Age at Death _____
- Place of Death _____
- Names of Parents _____
- Name of Spouse _____

For what purpose is information required? _____

What is your relationship to person whose record is requested? _____

In what capacity are you acting? _____

SIGNATURE OF APPLICANT _____ DATE _____

ADDRESS _____

Send record to: (please print)
- Name _____
- Address _____
- City _____ State _____ Zip Code _____

If requesting birth and marriage records, please sign the following statement:
To the best of my knowledge, the person(s) named in the application are deceased.

SIGNATURE OF APPLICANT _____

DOH - 1562 (10/91) p. 1 of 2

Health Commissioner's Administrative Rules and Regulations
Summary

1. Genealogical Research

Uncertified copies or abstracts from records of birth, death, and marriage may be provided for genealogical research purposes subject to the restrictions specified in this summary. All requests must be submitted in writing and include payment of the applicable statutory fee. The applicant shall be required to pay the specified fee for the time spent for the search and uncertified copy or notification of no record.

2. Who is authorized to do the searching?

Record searches shall be conducted only by the following persons in the files maintained by their respective agencies:

a. authorized employees of the State Department of Health;
b. a local registrar, deputy registrar, or an authorized employee of the registrar;
c. a town or city clerk, deputy clerk, or an authorized employee of the town or city clerk.

3. What records are available?

a. No information shall be released from a record of birth which has been placed in a confidential file pursuant to Public Health Law Section 4138.
b. No information shall be released from a record of birth unless the record has been on file for at least 75 years and the person to whom the record relates is known to the applicant to be deceased.
c. No information shall be released from a record of death unless the record has been on file for at least 50 years.
d. No information shall be released from a record of marriage unless the record has been on file for at least 50 years and the parties to the marriage are known to the applicant to be deceased.
e. The time periods specified in (3B), (3C), and (3D) are waived if the applicant is a descendant or has been designated to act on behalf of a descendant of the person whose record is being requested. A descendant is a person in the direct line of descent. The applicant shall provide documentation of descendancy prior to the release of information in those instances where a waiver of the waiting period is requested. A party acting on behalf of a descendant shall further provide documentation that the descendant authorized the party to make such application.
f. All uncertified copies, abstracts, or information issued for genealogical research purposes shall be clearly marked with the statement "For Genealogical Purposes Only."

4. Genealogy Fee Schedule

Fee schedule per one spelling of name. Fee varies depending on requested number of years to be searched. Unused fees will be refunded.

Years	Fee	Years	Fee
1-3 years	$11.00	31-40 years	$51.00
4-10 years	$21.00	41-50 years	$61.00
11-20 years	$31.00	51-60 years	$71.00
21-30 years	$41.00	61-70 years	$81.00

New York State Department of Health
A Verified Transcript from the Register of Live Births

District Number _____ Registered Number _____

Place of Birth _____
Town
Village _____
City

Hospital or Street _____

Full Name of Child _____

Date of Birth _____

Sex _____ Single _____ Twin Number _____

Name of Father _____

Color or Race _____ Age _____ Yrs.

Birthplace of Father _____

Usual Occupation _____

Maiden Name of Mother _____

Residence of Mother _____

Town
Village _____
City

Color or Race _____

Birthplace of Mother _____

Usual Occupation _____

Number of Other Children: Now Living _____ Now Dead _____

Medical Attendant _____

Address _____

Date Birth Certificate Filed _____

Date and Location of Transcript _____

Official and Title _____

Repository _____; Film number _____; Volume and page _____; Date researched _____; Copy of original made _____?; Researcher's Notes:

PLACE OF REGISTRY
STATE OF NEW YORK
County_____
City_____

New York State Department of Health
Division of Vital Statistics

Marriage License

Registered No._____

Know all Men by this Certificate, that any person authorized by law to perform marriage ceremonies within the State of New York to whom this may come, he, nor knowing any lawful impediment thereto, is hereby authorized and empowered to solemnize the rites of matrimony between_____

in the County of _____ and State of New York and _____

in the County of _____ and State of New York and to certify the same to be said parties or either of them under his hand and seal in his ministerial or official capacity and thereupon he is required to return his certificate in the form hereto annexed. The statement endorsed hereon or annexed hereto, by me subscribed, contain a full and true abstract of all the facts concerning such parties disclosed by their affidavits or verified statements presented to me upon the application for this license.

In Testimony Whereof, I have hereunto set my hand and affixed the seal of said City at the Municipal Building this _____ day of _____ nineteen hundred and _____.

{SEAL}

_____
City Clerk

The following is a full and true abstract of all the facts disclosed by the above-named applicants in their verified statements presented to me upon their applications for the above license.

FROM THE GROOM:

Full name_____

Color_____
Place of residence_____

Age_____
Occupation_____
Place of birth_____
Name of father_____

Country of birth_____
Maiden name of mother_____

Country of birth_____
Number of marriage_____
I have not to my knowledge been infected with any
  venereal disease, or if I have been so infected
  within five years I have had a laboratory test
  within that period which shows that I am now
  free from infection from any such disease.
Former wife or wives
living or dead_____
Is applicant a divorced person_____
If so, when and where divorce or divorces were granted_____

FROM THE BRIDE:

Full name_____

Color_____
Place of residence_____

Age_____
Occupation_____
Place of birth_____
Name of father_____

Country of birth_____
Maiden name of mother_____

Country of birth_____
Number of marriage_____
I have not to my knowledge been infected with any
  venereal disease, or if I have been so infected
  within five years I have had a laboratory test
  within that period which shows that I am now
  free from infection from any such disease.
Former husband or husbands
living or dead_____
Is applicant a divorced person_____
If so, when and where divorce or divorces were granted_____

Repository _____; Film number _____; Volume and page _____; Date researched _____; Copy of original made _____?; Researcher's Notes:

A Selection of Reproducible Genealogy Forms and Tips for Using Them

New York State Department of Health, Office of Vital Statistics
Certificate of Death

Dist. No. _____ Registered No. _____
1. Place of Death, State of New York: (a) County _____ ; (b) Town _____ ; (c) City or Village _____ ; (d) Name of Hospital or Institution _____ ; (e) Length of Stay in Town, City, or Village _____ .
2. Usual Residence: (a) State _____ ; (b) County _____ ; (c) Town _____ ; (d) Street Address _____ .
3. Name of Deceased _____ .
4. Date of Death _____ .
5. Sex _____ .
6. Color or Race _____ .
7. Single, Married, Widowed, Divorced _____ .
8. If Married, Widowed, or Divorced, Name of Husband or Wife _____ .
9. Date of Birth _____ .
10. Age _____ .
11. Birthplace (State or Foreign Country) _____ .
12. Citizen of What Country _____ .
13. (a) Usual Occupation _____ ;
    (b) Kind of Business or Industry _____ .
14. Father's Name _____ .
15. Mother's Maiden Name _____ .
16. Was Deceased Ever in U.S. Armed Forces? Yes/No;
    If yes, year or dates of service _____ .
17. Social Security Number _____ .
18. Informant's Name _____ ; Address _____ .

Medical Certification:
19. [I] Disease or Condition Directly Leading to Death:

    Cause of Death   Interval Between Disease and Death

    (A) _____   _____
    due to
    (B) _____   _____
    due to
    (C) _____   _____
    [II] Other Significant Conditions
    _____   _____

20. (a) Date of Operation _____ ; (b) Major Findings of Operation;
21. Autopsy? Yes/No
22. (a) Accident/Suicide/Homicide; (b) Place of Injury _____ ; (c) Where Did Injury Occur _____ ; (d) Time _____ ; (e) Injury Occurred At Work/Not at Work; (f) How Did Injury Occur _____ .
23. I hereby certify that I attended the deceased from _____ , 19 ___ , to _____ , 19 ___ ; that I last saw the deceased alive on _____ , 19 ___ ; and that death occurred at _____ , 19 ___ , from the causes and on the date stated above.
24. (a) Signature _____ M.D.; (b) _____ ; (c) Date Signed _____ , 19 ___ .
25. (a) Place of Burial, Cremation, or Removal _____ ; (b) Date _____ , 19 ___ ;
    (c) Undertaker's Signature _____ License No. _____ ; (d) Address _____ .
26. Date Filed by Local Reg. _____ , 19 ___ .
27. Registrar's Signature _____ .
    Burial or Transit: Permit Issued By _____ ; Date of Issue _____ , 19 ___ .

Repository _____ ; Film number _____ ; Volume and page _____ ; Date researched _____ ; Copy of original made _____ ?; Researcher's Notes:

Part III

New York City Records

New York City Vital Records

This section is organized differently from the other sections because there are several different City agencies that issue original and archival records. The information given here provides only general guidance. Complete information about all locations in New York City that can provide access to vital records or indexes to them is in Guzik, *Genealogical Resources in the New York Metropolitan Area*. This book is becoming dated, however, and it is best to phone first to determine availability of years and prices.

Forms Provided

Department of Health, Division of Vital Records
    A.   *The City of New York — Department of Health: Application for a Birth Record.*
    B.   *The City of New York — Department of Health: Application for a Death Record.*

Department of Records and Information Services, Municipal Archives
    C.   *Genealogy Collections*
    D.   *Application for a Search and/or Certified Copy of a Birth Record*
    E.   *Application for a Search and/or Certified Copy of a Marriage Record*
    F.   *Application for a Search and/or Certified Copy of a Death Record*
    G.   *Certificate and Record of Birth*
    H.   *Certificate and Record of Marriage*
    I.   *Certificate and Record of Death (ca. 1928)*
    J.   *Certificate and Record of Death (ca. 1936)*
    K.   *Certificate and Record of Death (ca. 1946)*
    L.   *Certificate and Record of Death (ca. 1989)*

New York City Marriage License Bureau
    M.   *In-Person Request for Marriage Record Search and Transcript* (can also be used for a search by mail)

What Records Are Available

In contrast to most of the rest of New York State, New York City issued its own birth, marriage, and death records, although these usually are on forms virtually identical to the State forms. Copies can be provided with various restrictions from the sources listed below. Many older holdings have been filmed by the Family History Library and can be found cataloged under New York, New York (City)—Vital Records and are listed in the JewishGen InfoFile below.

Birth
Birth records are issued by the Department of Health. The New York City Municipal Archives has birth records for all boroughs for the years 1847-1909 and indexes for 1857-1909; these are available with no restrictions. The Health Department has records and indexes for 1910 through the present; indexes are available for public use; records are not open, and availability is highly restricted.

Marriage
For the years 1908 to 1937, New York City issued two types of marriage certificates, one by the Department of Health and the other by the City Clerk in the borough where the marriage took place. The Municipal Archives has fully accessible Department of Health records and brides indexes for all boroughs for the years 1866-1937. The City Clerk, Manhattan, has Manhattan City Clerk's records 1908-41 and indexes for all boroughs, 1908-72, and Bronx and Queens Health Department records for 1898-1937. (The New York Public Library, Microforms Division, has Health Department grooms index for 1898-1937.) For marriages that took place in one of the five boroughs of NYC, contact the City Clerk's office in the borough in which the marriage certificate was obtained

(see addresses, below). One exception to this is that marriage certificates older than 1898 from Queens and Richmond counties are on file in the office of the New York State Department of Health. For help in locating the correct office, contact the Manhattan City Clerk's office at 212-669-8090 or by writing to them at the following address: New York City Clerk, Manhattan Office, Municipal Building, 1 Centre Street, Room 252, New York, NY 10007.

Death

Death records are issued by the Department of Health, Division of Vital Records. The New York City Municipal Archives has death records for all boroughs for the years 1795–1948 and indexes for 1848–1948. The Health Department has records and indexes for 1910 through the present; indexes are available for public use; records are not open.

There have been numerous changes in the form of death records used over the past 100 years. The four provided here are replicas of Department of Health Certificates used in (1) 1928, (2) 1936, (3) 1946, and (4) 1989. Most of the changes are in format; there are relatively few differences in the required information. Other format changes have occurred in intervening years, as well, but differences are small. These forms should cover most instances. Informant information appears on the front of the form in some formats and on the back in others. The 1946 format (No. 3) requests a significant amount of information that may also be requested in other years.

Where to Find Them

New York City Department of Records and Information Services, Municipal Archives, 31 Chambers Street, Room 103, New York, NY 10007, (212) 788-8580.

City Clerk's Office, Manhattan Marriage License Bureau, Municipal Building, 1 Centre Street, Room 252, New York, NY 10007, (212) 669-8170. Manhattan City Clerk marriage records are available from 1908 to the present. (Includes the Bronx, 1908–13). (Note: This is only for the City Clerk's records; a parallel set of records maintained by the Health Department 1908–37 are available from the Municipal Archives.)

City Clerk's Office, Bronx Marriage License Bureau, 1780 Grand Concourse, 2nd Floor, Bronx, NY 19457, (212) 731-2277. Bronx City Clerk's records are available from 1914 to the present.

City Clerk's Office, Brooklyn Marriage License Bureau, Municipal Building, Room 205, 210 Joralemon Street, Brooklyn, NY 11201, (718) 802-3581. Brooklyn City Clerk's records are available from 1908 to the present.

Queens City Clerk's Office, Marriage License Bureau, Queens City Hall, 120-55 Queens Boulevard, Kew Gardens, NY 11424, (718) 520-3665. Queens City Clerk's records are available from 1881 to the present.

Richmond City Clerk's Office, Marriage License Bureau, Borough Hall, 10 Richmond Terrace, Room 311, Staten Island, NY 10301, (718) 390-5175 or 5176. Richmond (Staten Island) record's are available from 1908 to the present.

New York City Department of Health, Bureau of Vital Records, 125 Worth Street, Room 133, New York, NY 10013, (212) 566-8193 or (212) 566-8194. Records can be ordered by phone with a credit card. (Birth records for all New York City boroughs, 1898 to present. Birth records are available only to the individual or a direct descendant. Death records 1930 to present. Information on other restrictions and requirements is available from the source.)

What You Need Before You Search

1. Approximate date of event
2. For marriages, there may be separate indexes for brides and grooms.

3. Preferably borough. (Most early records are indexed by borough or localities which later became part of New York City; later years use consolidated indexes for all five boroughs. For brides residing outside of New York City, the record was filed where the license was obtained. After 1943: all marriage certificates were filed in the borough where the couple obtained their license.)

Tips (on using Municipal Archives)

- The request forms shown are reproductions of the forms provided by the Municipal Archives. The originals are in color:
  Birth: Beige
  Marriage: Pink
  Death: Green
- The prices are the same whether requesting by mail or in person, i.e., you can do the search yourself or they'll do it for you. This office responds quickly to mail requests; it usually takes only two-three weeks to receive a reply. If requesting in person, a copy can be obtained in a few minutes, depending on how busy they are.
- The design of record forms has changed slightly over the last 100 years, but the information collected is essentially the same. These replicas should enable the recording of all the information,
- Certified copies are made by the clerks from the same microfilm records used by the public. Although a reader/printer is available for public use, its use for copying vital records is not permitted. Only the staff can copy these records and certify them.
- The microfilmed records contain all the information on the originals. The one known exception is that the originals of the death records—but not the microfilmed copies—contain the name and address of the informant. If this added information is desired, a special request can be made to have a copy of the original provided. It usually will be mailed later.

Tips (on using City Clerk's Office)

- There are specific restrictions on the availability of records; for genealogical purposes, they are generally available only to the couple or their authorized representatives.
- Records for the years indicated are available only from the boroughs in which the record was filed. Earlier records for the entire city are available from the New York City Municipal Archives.
- Indexes can be accessed only by the clerks, not researchers. Each borough office has indexes for that borough.
- For years 1908-71, the City Clerk's Office has alphabetical ledger indexes for both brides and grooms. For 1972 and later, the lists are computerized.

Tips (on using Health Department records)

- There are book indexes for each year. Other indexes are available for earlier years. In-person use may be restricted.

Additional Help

Family History Library, *Research Outline, New York*, Series US-STATES no. 32 (Salt Lake City, UT: The Genealogical Department, Church of Jesus Christ of Latter Day Saints, March 1992).

Guzik, *Genealogical Resources in the New York Metropolitan Area*, pp. 59-68.

JewishGen InfoFile," New York City Birth, Marriage and Death Records,"
<http://www.jewishgen.org>, Jan. 1996.

Kronman, Barbara, *The Guide to New York City Public Records,* *(New York:* Public Interest Clearinghouse, 4th edition, 1992).

Polakoff, Eileen, "The Golden Door: Genealogical Research in New York City, *Avotaynu,* vol. XI, No. 3, Fall 1995.

NO PERSONAL CHECKS

THE CITY OF NEW YORK – DEPARTMENT OF HEALTH

DIVISION OF VITAL RECORDS
P.O. Box 3776
Church Street Station
New York, N.Y. 10007

APPLICATION FOR A BIRTH RECORD
(Print All Items Clearly)

LAST NAME ON BIRTH RECORD	FIRST NAME	☐ FEMALE ☐ MALE
DATE OF BIRTH — Month Day Year	PLACE OF BIRTH (NAME OF HOSPITAL, OR IF AT HOME, NO. AND STREET)	BOROUGH OF BIRTH
MOTHER'S MAIDEN NAME (Name Before Marriage) — FIRST LAST	CERTIFICATE NUMBER IF KNOWN	
FATHER'S NAME — FIRST LAST	*For Office Use Only*	
NO. OF COPIES	YOUR RELATIONSHIP TO PERSON NAMED ON BIRTH RECORD. IF SELF, STATE "SELF"	
FOR WHAT PURPOSE ARE YOU GOING TO USE THIS BIRTH RECORD		

NOTE: Copy of a birth record can be issued only to persons to whom the record of birth relates, if of age, or a parent or other lawful representative. IF THIS REQUEST IS NOT FOR YOUR OWN BIRTH RECORD OR THAT OF YOUR CHILD, NOTARIZED AUTHORIZATION FROM THE PARENT OR THE PERSON NAMED ON THE CERTIFICATE MUST BE PRESENTED WITH THIS APPLICATION.

Section 3.19, New York City Health Code provides, in part: "... no person shall make a false, untrue or misleading statement or forge the signature of another on a certificate, application, registration, report or other document required to be prepared pursuant to this Code." Section 558 (d) of the New York City Charter provides that any violation of the Health Code shall be treated and punished as a misdemeanor.

SIGN YOUR NAME AND ADDRESS BELOW

NAME
ADDRESS
CITY   STATE   ZIP CODE

NOTE: PLEASE ATTACH A STAMPED SELF-ADDRESSED ENVELOPE

FEES

SEARCH FOR TWO CONSECUTIVE YEARS AND ONE COPY OR A CERTIFIED "NOT FOUND STATEMENT" $15.00
EACH ADDITIONAL COPY REQUESTED $15.00
EACH EXTRA YEAR SEARCHED (WITH THIS APPLICATION) .... $ 3.00
1. Make certified check or money order payable to: Department of Health, N.Y.C.
2. If from a foreign country, send an international money order or a certified check drawn on a U.S. Bank.
3. Stamps or foreign currency will not be accepted. CASH NOT ACCEPTED BY MAIL.

FOR OFFICE USE ONLY

SEARCH RESULTS →	REPORTED BY ☐ CRT ☐ MANUAL →	CERTIFICATE NUMBER	LAST NAME - 4 LETTERS	DATE OF BIRTH — Month Day Year
	READING DATE	DATE ISSUED: BY MAIL	DATE ISSUED: IN PERSON	

VR-67 (REV. 6/91)

SEE INSTRUCTIONS ON REVERSE

TO REQUEST BIRTH CERTIFICATE IN PERSON

Persons requesting a birth certificate should complete the application (see reverse side) and go to the cashier's window.

If you desire your own certificate or your child's certificate and if you have proper identification such as driver's license or an employee identification card you may receive the certificate immediately. Otherwise, it will be mailed to you within a few days.

Please have the $15.00 fee (no personal checks) and your identification ready when you go to the window.

TO REQUEST BIRTH CERTIFICATE BY MAIL

Persons requesting a birth certificate should complete the application (see reverse side).

Return completed application with certified check or money order in the amount of $15.00 (no personal checks).

Mail to: P.O. Box 3776, Church Street Station, New York 10007.

INSTRUCCIONES PARA SOLICITAR UN CERTIFICADO DE NACIMIENTO EN PERSONA

Personas que soliciten certificados de nacimiento deben llenar la aplicación (ver al dorso) y pagar en la ventanilla del cajero.

Si usted desea obtener su propio certificado o el de su hijo(a) y tiene la debida documentación: licencia de conducir o una tarjeta de identidad de su lugar de empleo, podrá recibir el certificado inmediatamente. Si no tuviera la debida documentación, el certificado se le enviará por correo.

Por favor tenga los $15.00 dólares (no cheques personales) y su identificación a mano cuando vaya a la ventanilla del cajero.

INSTRUCCIONES PARA SOLICITAR UN CERTIFICADO DE NACIMIENTO POR CORREO

Personas que soliciten certificados de nacimiento por correo deben llenar la aplicación (ver al dorso) y enviarla con un cheque certificado o giro postal por la cantidad de $15.00 dólares (no cheques personales) a la siguiente dirección: P.O. Box 3776, Church Street Station, New York 10007.

NO PERSONAL CHECKS

THE CITY OF NEW YORK – DEPARTMENT OF HEALTH
DIVISION OF VITAL RECORDS
P.O. Box 3776
Church Street Station
New York, N.Y. 10007

APPLICATION FOR A COPY OF A DEATH RECORD
(Print All Items Clearly)

1. LAST NAME AT TIME OF DEATH	2. FIRST NAME	2.A ☐ FEMALE ☐ MALE
3. DATE OF DEATH Month Day Year	4. PLACE OF DEATH	5. BOROUGH	6. AGE
7. NO OF COPIES	8. SPOUSE'S NAME	9. OCCUPATION OF DECEASED
10. FATHER'S NAME	11. SOCIAL SECURITY NUMBER
12. MOTHER'S NAME (Name Before Marriage)	13. BURIAL PERMIT NUMBER (IF KNOWN)
14. FOR WHAT PURPOSE ARE YOU GOING TO USE THIS CERTIFICATE	15. YOUR RELATIONSHIP TO DECEDENT

NOTE: Section 205.07 of the Health Code provides, in part:" . . . The confidential medical report of death shall not be subject to subpoena or to inspection." Therefore, copies of the medical report of death cannot be issued.

SIGN YOUR NAME AND ADDRESS BELOW

NAME
ADDRESS
CITY   STATE   ZIP CODE

INFORMATION: APPLICATION SHOULD BE MADE IN PERSON AT 125 WORTH STREET OR BY MAIL TO THE ABOVE DIVISION.

NOTE:
1. CASH NOT ACCEPTED BY MAIL
2. PLEASE ATTACH A STAMPED SELF-ADDRESSED ENVELOPE

FEES

(FOR OFFICE USE ONLY)

SEARCH FOR TWO CONSECUTIVE YEARS AND ONE COPY $15.00
EACH ADDITIONAL COPY REQUESTED $15.00
EACH EXTRA YEAR SEARCHED (WITH THIS APPLICATION) .... $ 3.00
IF RECORD IS NOT ON FILE, A CERTIFIED "NOT FOUND STATEMENT" WILL BE ISSUED.

1. Make certified check or money order payable to: Department of Health, N.Y.C.
2. If from a foreign country, send an international money order or a certified check drawn on a U.S. Bank.
3. Stamps or foreign currency will not be accepted.

MAIL REQUESTS TO:
Department of Health, Division of Vital Records
P.O. Box 3776, Church Street Station, New York City, N.Y. 10007

VR-66 (REV. 6/91)

N.Y.C. DEPARTMENT OF RECORDS AND INFORMATION SERVICES
MUNICIPAL ARCHIVES
31 CHAMBERS STREET - ROOM 103, NEW YORK, NY 10007
(212) 788-8580

GENEALOGY COLLECTIONS

All of the records described below are available for research in the Municipal Archives Reference Room, open Monday to Thursday, 9 a.m. to 4:30 p.m.; Friday, 9 a.m. to 1 p.m. Search service via mail is available for vital records and the 1890 New York City census only. Please consult application forms for search and copy fee information.

VITAL RECORDS - Birth, death and marriage records are filed and indexed according to the locality (Borough) in which the event occurred. The following is a list of existing records for each borough.

MANHATTAN	Births	July 1847 - 1848; July 1853 - 1909
	Deaths	1795; 1802 - 1804; 1808; 1812 - 1948
	Marriages*	June 1847 - 1848; July 1853 - 1937
BROOKLYN	Births	1866 - 1909
	Deaths	1847 - 1853; 1857 - 1948
	Marriages*	1866 - 1937
BRONX	Births	1898 - 1909
	Deaths	1898 - 1948
	Marriages*	1898 - 1937

The Bronx did not exist as separate Borough until 1898. Before then, the Bronx was part of Westchester County, except for certain western areas which were annexed by New York (Manhattan) in 1874, and eastern areas annexed in 1895. For vital records in those areas and years, request a search for <u>Manhattan</u>.

QUEENS	Births	1898 - 1909
	Deaths	1898 - 1948
	Marriages*	1898 - 1937
	Town and Village Vital Records, 1847-1849; 1871-1898	
RICHMOND (Staten Island)	Births	1898 - 1909
	Deaths	1898 - 1948
	Marriages*	1898 - 1937
	Town and Village Vital Records, 1847-1849; 1881-1897	

CENSUS

MANHATTAN   1890 New York City (MANHATTAN ONLY) "Police Census." Listed according to address the census recorded the name, age and sex of each resident, including children.

BROOKLYN   New York State Census, Kings County, 1855, 1865, 1875, 1892, 1905, 1915. Not indexed; listed according to Ward, Assembly and Election District number. Recorded name, family relationship, sex, age, nativity, occupation, and citizenship status. No mail search service.

RICHMOND   New York State Census, Richmond County, 1855, 1865, 1870, 1875, 1880, 1915, 1925. Not indexed; similar information recorded as Kings County Census. No mail search service.

CITY DIRECTORY   Manhattan: 1873-1913; 1915-1918; 1920; 1922; 1924; 1931; 1933
Brooklyn: 1796; 1802; 1811; 1822-1826; 1829-1910; 1912-1913; 1933

Listed alphabetically, by last name, head of household (male adults primarily; women usually only if widowed), his or her occupation, home address and/or business address. No mail search service.

*Health Department marriage certificates and indexes for all Boroughs prior to 1938 are available on microfilm. Index to City Clerk marriage licenses for all Boroughs, 1908 through 1929, available on microfilm; licenses 1908-1929 have not been microfilmed; license copies available via special order only.

A Selection of Reproducible Genealogy Forms and Tips for Using Them

**NEW YORK CITY
DEPARTMENT OF RECORDS AND INFORMATION SERVICES
MUNICIPAL ARCHIVES**
31 Chambers Street
New York, N.Y. 10007
(212) 566-5292

BIRTH

APPLICATION FOR A SEARCH AND/OR CERTIFIED COPY OF A BIRTH RECORD:

FEES

$10.00	Search of birth records in one year and one City/Borough for one name and issuance of one certified copy or "not found" statement.
$ 2.00	Per additional year to be searched in one City/Borough for same name.
$ 2.00	Per additional City/Borough to be searched in one year for same name.
$ 5.00	Per additional copy of record.
$ 5.00	Issuance of certified copy, when certificate number is provided.

Enclose stamped, self-addressed envelope.

Make check or money order payable to: NYC Department of Records.

PLEASE PRINT OR TYPE:

Last name on birth record	First name	Female/Male

Date of birth

Month	Day	Year	
Place of birth – if at home, house number and street			City/Borough

Father's name, if known	Mother's name, if known

Your relationship to person named above	Certificate no., if known

Purpose for which this record will be used	Number of copies requested

Your name, please print	Signature

Address

City	State	Zip Code

MA-22 (9-90)

**NEW YORK CITY
DEPARTMENT OF RECORDS AND INFORMATION SERVICES
MUNICIPAL ARCHIVES**
31 Chambers Street
New York, N.Y. 10007
(212) 566-5292

MARRIAGE

APPLICATION FOR A SEARCH AND/OR CERTIFIED COPY
OF A MARRIAGE RECORD:

FEES

$10.00	Search of marriage records in one year and one City/Borough for one Groom and/or Bride and issuance of one certified copy or "not found" statement.
$ 2.00	Per additional year to be searched in one City/Borough for same name.
$ 2.00	Per additional City/Borough to be searched in one year for same name.
$ 5.00	Per additional copy of record.
$ 5.00	Issuance of certified copy, when certificate number is provided.

Enclose stamped, self-addressed envelope.

Make check or money order payable to: NYC Department of Records.

PLEASE PRINT OR TYPE:

Last name of Groom	First name of Groom
Last name of Bride (Maiden name)	First name of Bride

Date of Marriage

Month	Day	Year(s)

Place of Marriage	City/Borough
Your relationship to people named above	Certificate no., if known
Purpose for which this record will be used	Number of copies requested
Your name, please print	Signature

Address

City	State	Zip Code

MA-25 (9-90)

**NEW YORK CITY
DEPARTMENT OF RECORDS AND INFORMATION SERVICES
MUNICIPAL ARCHIVES**
31 Chambers Street
New York, N.Y. 10007
(212) 566-5292

DEATH

APPLICATION FOR A SEARCH AND/OR CERTIFIED COPY OF A DEATH RECORD:

FEES

Fee	Description
$10.00	Search of death records in one year and one City/Borough for one name and issuance of one certified copy or "not found" statement.
$ 2.00	Per additional year to be searched in one City/Borough for same name.
$ 2.00	Per additional City/Borough to be searched in one year for same name.
$ 5.00	Per additional copy of record.
$ 5.00	Issuance of certified copy, when certificate number is provided.

Enclose stamped, self-addressed envelope.

Make check or money order payable to: NYC Department of Records.

PLEASE PRINT OR TYPE:

Last name at time of death	First name	Middle name

Date of death	Cemetery, if known	
Month Day Year		
Place of death	City/Borough	Age
Father's name, if known	Mother's name, if known	

Your relationship to decedent	Certificate no., if known
Purpose for which this record will be used	Number of copies requested

Your name, please print	Signature

Address

City	State	Zip Code

MA-23 (9-90)

Certificate No._____

City of New York
Certificate and Record of Birth
of

Name of Child _____

Child		Father's Occupation	
Color		Mother's Name	
Date of Birth		Mother's Name Before Marriage	
Place of Birth Street and No.		Mother's Residence	
Father's Name		Mother's Birthplace	
Father's Residence		Mother's Age	
Father's Birthplace		Number of Previous Children	
Father's Age		How Many Now Living in All	

Signature_____

Date of Report_____

Repository_____; Film number _____; Volume and page_____; Date researched _____; Copy of original made _____?; Researcher's Notes:

A Selection of Reproducible Genealogy Forms and Tips for Using Them • 91

Certificate No. _____

City of New York
Certificate and Record of Marriage
of

_____ and _____
(Groom's Full Name)   (Bride's Full Name)

Groom's Residence		Bride's Residence	
Age		Age	
Color		Color	
Single, Widowed, or Divorced		Single, Widowed, or Divorced	
Occupation		Maiden Name if a Widow	
Birthplace		Birthplace	
Father's Name		Father's Name	
Mother's Maiden Name		Mother's Maiden Name	
No. of Groom's Marriage		No. of Bride's Marriage	

I hereby certify that the above-named groom and bride were joined in Marriage by me, in accordance with the Laws of the State of New York, at _____, in the Borough of _____, City of New York, this _____ of _____ 19____.

Signature of
person performing
the Ceremony _____
Official Station _____
Residence _____
Date of Record _____

Witnesses to the _____
Marriage   _____
Witnesses to the _____
Certification   _____

Repository _____ ; Film number _____ ; Volume and page _____ ; Date researched _____ ; Copy of original made _____?; Researcher's Notes:

STATE OF NEW YORK
Department of Health of The City of New York
Bureau of Records
STANDARD CERTIFICATE OF DEATH (ca. 1928)

1. PLACE OF DEATH
BOROUGH OF _____
No. _____ St.
(If institution, state name)

Character of premises
whether tenement,
private, hotel, etc. _____

REGISTERED NO _____

2. FULL NAME _____

3. SEX	4. COLOR OR RACE	5. SINGLE, MARRIED, WIDOWED, OR DIVORCED (write the word)

15. DATE OF DEATH
_____ 19____
(Month)   (Day)   (Year)

6. DATE OF BIRTH
_____
(Month)   (Day)   (Year)

16 *I hereby certify that the foregoing particulars (Nos. 1 to 15 inclusive) are correct as near as the same can be ascertained, and I further certify that I have this _____ day of _____ 19____, taken charge of the body of deceased found at _____ and that I have investigated the essential facts concerning the circumstances of the death.*

7. AGE
_____ yrs _____ mos. _____ da.

If less than 1
day, ____ hrs.
or ____ min?

8. OCCUPATION
(a. Trade, profession, or particular kind of work _____
(b) General nature of industry, business or establishment in which employed (or employer) . _____

17 *I further certify that I have viewed said body and from_____ and evidence, that __he died on the _____ day of _____ 192____, at ____M., and that the chief and determining cause of ____ death was _____*

_____ that
the contributing causes were _____

9. BIRTHPLACE   (State or country)

(9). How long in (A) U.S. (if of foreign birth)	(9) How long resi- (B) dent in City of New York?

PARENTS OF DECEASED
10. NAME OF FATHER

11. BIRTHPLACE OF FATHER
(State or country)

_____
Assistant Medical Examiner

12. MAIDEN NAME OF MOTHER

13. BIRTHPLACE OF MOTHER
(State or country)

14. Special INFORMATION required in deaths in hospitals and institutions and in deaths of non-residents and recent residents
Former or
usual residence _____

Approved

_____
Chief Medical Examiner

FILED	18. PLACE OF BURIAL	DATE OF BURIAL _____ 19____
	19. UNDERTAKER	ADDRESS

Repository _____ ; Film number _____ ; Volume and page _____ ; Date researched _____ ; Copy of original made _____ ?; Researcher's Notes:

A Selection of Reproducible Genealogy Forms and Tips for Using Them • 93

STATE OF NEW YORK
Department of Health of The City of New York
Bureau of Records
STANDARD CERTIFICATE OF DEATH (ca. 1936)
REGISTERED NO_____

1. PLACE OF DEATH
BOROUGH OF_____
No._____St._____
Character of premises: whether tenement, private, hotel, etc._____

2. PRINT FULL NAME_____

3. SEX	4. COLOR OR RACE	5. SINGLE, MARRIED, WIDOWED, OR DIVORCED (write the word)	15. DATE OF DEATH _____ 19___ (Month) (Day) (Year)
5A. WIFE/ HUSBAND } OF			16 *I hereby certify that the foregoing particulars (Nos. 1 to 14 inclusive) are correct as near as the same can be ascertained, and I further certify that*
6. DATE OF BIRTH OF DECEDENT (Month) (Day) (Year)			
8. AGE OF DECEDENT ____yrs ____mos. ____da.		If less than 1 day,____hrs. or ____min?	*I attended the deceased from* _____, 19_____, to _____, 19____; *that I last saw* ____ *alive on the ____ day of _____ 19___, That death occurred on the date stated above, at_____ ____m.*
8. OCCUPATION A. Trade, profession, or particular kind of work _____ B. General nature of industry, business or establishment in which employed (or employer) ._____			*and that the cause of death was as follows:* _____ _____ _____ _____
9. BIRTHPLACE (State or country)			
(9). How long in (A) U.S. (if of foreign birth)	(9) How long resi- (B) dent in City of New York?		____duration ____yrs ____mos ____ds
PARENTS OF DECEASED 10. NAME OF FATHER OF DECEDENT			
11. BIRTHPLACE OF FATHER OF DECEDENT			Contributory_____ (Secondary)
12. MAIDEN NAME OF MOTHER OF DECEDENT			Operation?_____State kind_____ _____
13. BIRTHPLACE OF MOTHER (State or country)			____duration ____yrs ____mos ____ds
14. Special INFORMATION required in deaths in hospitals and institutions and in deaths of non-residents and recent residents Usual residence_____			Witness my hand this ____ day of ____, 19___
14A. INFORMANT			Signature_____ Address_____
FILED	17. PLACE OF BURIAL		DATE OF BURIAL_____ 19___
	18. UNDERTAKER		ADDRESS

Repository _____ ; Film number _____ ; Volume and page _____ ; Date researched _____ ; Copy of original made _____ ?; Researcher's Notes:

94 • *Documents of Our Ancestors*

STATE OF NEW YORK
Department of Health of The City of New York
Bureau of Records Certificate of Death (ca. 1946)

Certificate No._____

1. NAME OF DECEASED_____
   (Print or Typewriter)   First Name   Maiden Name   Last Name   Social Security Number

PERSONAL PARTICULARS (To be filled in by Funeral Director)	MEDICAL CERTIFICATE OF DEATH (To be filled in by Physician)
2. USUAL RESIDENCE: (a) State_____ (c) Post Office (b) Co._____ and Zone_____ (d) No._____ Ave. St. (If in rural area, give location) (e) Length of residence or stay in City of New York immediately prior to death	16. PLACE OF DEATH (a) NEW YORK CITY: (b) Borough_____ (c) Name of hospital or Institution_____ (If not in hospital or institution, give street and number) (d) Length of stay at place of death immediately prior to death
3. SINGLE, MARRIED, WIDOWED OR DIVORCED (write the word)	17. DATE AND HOUR (Month) (Day) (Year) (Hour) OF DEATH
4. WIFE } OF HUSBAND }	18. SEX | 19. COLOR OR RACE | 20. Approximate Age
5. DATE OF BIRTH (Month) (Day) Year OF DECEDENT	21. I HEREBY CERTIFY That (I attended the deceased) (a staff physician of this institution attended the deceased) from_____, 19____,
6. AGE yrs. mos. days | 7. If less than 1 day: hrs. or mins	to_____, 19____; and last saw him/her alive at _____, on_____ 19__ Statement of cause of death is based on (autopsy) (operation) (laboratory test) (clinical findings) *(Cross out items that do not apply)*
7. OCCUPATION A. Trade, profession, or particular kind of work done, as spinner, sawyer, bookkeeper, etc. B. Industry or business in which work was done, as silk mill, sawmill, bank, own business, etc.	Principal cause of death _____ | Date of Onset _____
8. BIRTHPLACE OF DECEDENT: (a) State_____ (c) City, Town (b) County or Village	
9. OF WHAT COUNTRY WAS DECEDENT A CITIZEN AT TIME OF DEATH?	Contributory causes and other conditions _____
10. WAS DECEASED WAR VETERAN. IF SO, NAME WAR	
PARENTS OF DECEASED 11. NAME OF FATHER OF DECEDENT	Autopsy: Date of_____ | Operation: Date of_____ (If none, so state) (If none, so state)
12. BIRTHPLACE OF FATHER (State or country)	Condition for which performed:_____
13. MAIDEN NAME OF MOTHER OF DECEDENT	Signature_____ M. D.
14. BIRTHPLACE OF MOTHER OF DECEDENT (State or country)	Address_____ Date_____

A Selection of Reproducible Genealogy Forms and Tips for Using Them

15. SIGNATURE OF INFORMANT	RELATIONSHIP TO DECEASED	ADDRESS	
22. PLACE OF BURIAL OR CREMATION		DATE OF BURIAL OR CREMATION	
23. FUNERAL DIRECTOR		ADDRESS	PERMIT NUMBER

FUNERAL DIRECTOR'S CERTIFICATE

I hereby certify that I have been employed, without any application on my part or that of any other person, to dispose of the remains of _____

by _____ of _____

who is the _____(Relationship)_____ and the nearest surviving relative or next of kin of the deceased.

Name of permittee _____ Permit No. _____

By _____
(Signature of licensed manager or funeral director if other than permittee.)

Must be Filled in by the Funeral Director When Obtaining Removal Permit by Telephone

Telephone Removal No. _____ granted by _____
                                           (A.M.)   (Burial Clerk)
Date _____ Hour _____ (P.M.) _____
                                                                          (Funeral Director)

Deaths that are even remotely associated with an earlier accident must be referred to the Medical Examiner.

Repository _____ ; Film number _____ ; Volume and page _____ ; Date researched _____ ; Copy of original made _____ ?; Researcher's Notes:

DATE FILED   CERTIFICATE OF DEATH (ca. 1989)

Certificate No._____

1. NAME OF DECEASED _____

(Type or Print)   (First Name)   (Middle Name)   (Last Name)

MEDICAL CERTIFICATE OF DEATH (To be filled in by the physician)

2. PLACE OF DEATH	2a. NEW YORK CITY ———— BOROUGH	2b. Name of hospital or other facility if not facility, street address	2c. If in Hospital or Other Facility (Check) 1 ☐ DOA 3 ☐ Outpatient 2 ☐ Emerg 4 ☐ Inpatient	2d. If Inpatient, date of current admission		
				Month	Day	Year

3a. Date and Hour of Death	(Month) (Day) (Year)	3b. HOUR	☐ AM ☐ PM	4. SEX	5 APPROXIMATE AGE

6. I HEREBY CERTIFY THAT: (Check One)
   ☐ I attended the deceased   ☐ A staff physician of this institution attended the deceased
   ☐ Dr._____ attended the deceased

   from_____ 19____. I further certify that traumatic injury or poisoning DID NOT play any part in causing death, and that death did not occur in any unusual manner and was due entirely to NATURAL CAUSES.

   Witness my hand this _____ day of _____ 19___ Signature_____ D.O. M.D.

   Name of Physician_____ Address_____

PERSONAL PARTICULARS (To be filled in by Funeral Director)

7. Usual Residence a. State	7b. County	7c. City, Town, or Location	7d. Street & House No. Zip. Apt. No	7e. Inside City Limits of 7c ☐ Yes ☐ No

8. Served in U.S. Armed Forces	9. Marital Status (Check One) 1 ☐ Never Married 2 ☐ Widowed 3 ☐ Married or separated 4 ☐ Divorced	10. Name of Surviving Spouse (If wife, give maiden name)

11. Date of birth (Month) (Day) (Year) of Decedent	12. Age at last birthday	If under 1 mos.	Year days	If less hours	than 1 day min.	13. Social Security No.

14a. Usual Occupation (Kind of work done during most of working lifetime, do not enter retired)	14b. Kind of Business

15. Birthplace (City & State or Foreign Country)	16. Education (Check only one) 0-11 12 13-15 16 17+ ☐ 1 ☐ 2 ☐ 3 ☐ 4 ☐ 5	17. Other name(s) by which decedent was known

18. NAME OF FATHER OF DECEDENT	19. MAIDEN NAME OF MOTHER OF DECEDENT

20a. NAME OF INFORMANT	20b. RELATIONSHIP TO DECEASED	20c. ADDRESS (City) (State) (Zip)

21a. NAME OF CEMETERY OR CREMATORY	21b. LOCATION (City, Town, State and Country)	21c. DATE OF BURIAL OR CREMATION

22a. FUNERAL DIRECTOR	22b. ADDRESS

Repository _____; Film number _____; Volume and page _____; Date researched _____; Copy of original made _____?; Researcher's Notes:

A Selection of Reproducible Genealogy Forms and Tips for Using Them • 97

The City of New York - Office of the City Clerk
Marriage License Bureau

IN-PERSON REQUEST FOR MARRIAGE RECORD SEARCH & TRANSCRIPT

NOTE: For records less than fifty (50) years old, a certified copy of the marriage record will only be released: a) to parties to the marriage; b) to persons presenting written authorization from one of the parties to the marriage; or c) to attorneys for litigation purposes. The reason that the search and transcript are needed must be indicated on the request form. Attorneys, upon their own stationery, must indicate the party or parties that they represent and the nature of any pending action, when making their request.

PRINT CLEARLY ALL INFORMATION BELOW

DATE:	
Date of Marriage Ceremony: Month: Day: Year:	Borough where the license was issued:
If uncertain, specify other years you want searched:	If known license number:
GROOM (man) Full Name:	Birth Date:
BRIDE (woman) Full MAIDEN Name:	Birth Date:
If woman was previously married, give LAST NAME of former husband (s):	
Reason search & copy are needed:	How many copies:
Name of person requesting search:	Your relationship to Bride & Groom:
Your Address City	State Zip

DO NOT WRITE BELOW — THIS SPACE FOR OFFICE USE

License Number:	Microfilm Cart Number:
Searched by:	Type of Cert:
Receipt No.: Amount $	Typist:
Date Complete:	Cert No. (s):

This is to certify that _____

residing at _____ Born _____

at _____ And _____

residing at _____ Born _____

at _____ by _____

Groom's Parents _____

Bride's Parents _____

Witnesses _____

Previous Marriages _____

REMARKS: _____

Form #IPSOO1F-40M (88)

New York City Voter Registration Form

Forms Provided

A. *Board of Elections in the City of New York, Brooklyn Borough Office, Application for Voting Information*
B. *Ledger Book Abstract Form*

(As far as is known, only the Brooklyn Borough Office uses a form, although a form is not necessary to request voter information. The same information can be requested without a form from any other borough.)

What is Available

New York City required annual voter registration until 1957. Most of the original registration forms still are available, although some early ones have been lost. The archived forms are copies of the actual voter applications. They have very useful genealogical data, and are an especially valuable alternative source for finding the court of naturalization when the person cannot be located in a court index or in the 1925 New York State Census.

As shown. registration forms generally include: name of registrant, country or state of birth, race, age, street address, marital status, length of residence in state/county/Assembly District and Election District, whether native born or naturalized, country of nativity; date of naturalization, court where naturalization occurred, and address where last voted.

There likely is similar data available from other cities' elections offices.

Where to Find Them

Board of Elections, Manhattan Borough Office, 200 Varick Street, 10th Floor, New York, NY 10014, (212) 886-3800. Manhattan voter records are available from 1916–20 (gaps) and 1923 to the present.

Board of Elections, Bronx Borough Office, 1780 Grand Concourse, Bronx, NY 10457, (212) 299-9017. Records are available from 1897 to the present.

Board of Elections, Brooklyn Borough Office, 345 Adams Street, 4th Floor, Brooklyn, NY 11201, (718) 330-2250. Brooklyn voter records are available from 1890 to the present.

Board of Elections, Queens Borough Office, 42-16 West Street, 2nd Floor, Long Island City, NY 11101, (718) 392-8989. Queens borough records are available from 1949 to the present.

Board of Elections, Staten Island Borough Office, 1 Edgewater Plaza, 4th Floor, Staten Island, NY 10305, (718) 876-0079. Staten Island borough records are available from 1957 to the present.

Municipal Archives has:
New York County: records of naturalized voters, 1872–78 and registers of voters, 1872–1922 (gaps).
Queens County: registers of voters, 1898–1948
Richmond County: registers of voters 1898–1956

What You Need Before You Search

The actual registration ledgers cannot be searched in person. The *List of Enrolled Voters* can be checked to determine if a person is registered in a given year. Year and address must be provided.

Tips

- Forms evidently are not needed if requesting records from the Municipal Archives or for Manhattan or the Bronx (but Kings County [Brooklyn] can provide records for all boroughs). The cost is $3.00 for searching one year for one address. Provide full name at registration, address where residing at the time of registration, date of birth or age.
- To verify that a person actually registered, *Lists of Enrolled Voters* are available at the Municipal Reference and Research Center (31 Chambers Street, Room 112, New York, NY 10007, (212) 566-4284) and the New York Public Library, Microforms Division. The latter is much more easily accessible.
- To use the *List of Enrolled Voters*, you must know the Assembly District (AD) and the Election District (ED); the New York Public Library, Map Division has AD/ED maps for New York City for most years (presidential election years are best). Maps also are available at the Municipal Reference and Research Center, or at the Board of Elections office of the appropriate boroughs.
- You can save the trouble of looking at the *Lists of Enrolled Voters,* a tedious and time-consuming process, by requesting the voter registration record from the Municipal Archives or the borough Board of Elections, and having the clerks do the searches. They'll inform you if the search was unsuccessful, and the cost is only $3.00.
- If your objective is to obtain naturalization information, your best bet is to search in presidential election years such as 1920 or 1932.
- After 1957, voters re-registered only when they changed addresses.
- In sending a request to a Borough Elections office, send a blank ledger book abstract form and ask that it be completed and returned to be sure you get full information.

Additional Help

Guzik, *Genealogical Resources in the New York Metropolitan Area*, pp. 8–9, 143–4; 158–9; 191–2; 211.

Form 1660-AG-91

MARIA ECHAVESTE, PRESIDENT
KATHLEEN M. WAGNER, SECRETARY
VINCENT J. CUTTITA
JEANNETTE GADSON
FERDINAND C. MARCHI
ALICE SACHS
ANTHONY SADOWSKI
GEORGE M. SPANAKOS
GERTRUDE STROHM
VINCENT J. VELELLA

COMMISSIONERS

BOARD OF ELECTIONS
IN
THE CITY OF NEW YORK

BROOKLYN BOROUGH OFFICE
345 ADAMS STREET
BROOKLYN, N. Y. 11201
(718) 330-2250

DANIEL DeFRANCESCO
EXECUTIVE DIRECTOR
ALFRED S. PANTALEONE
DEPUTY EXECUTIVE DIRECTOR
JON DEL GIORNO
ADMINISTRATIVE MANAGER
JAMES R. McMANUS
LEONARD WERTHEIM
SENIOR ADMINISTRATORS
WILLIAM J. CRO
DIRECTOR OF MANAGEMENT
INFORMATION SYSTEMS
SIDNEY F. STRAUSS
JOSEPH N. GIAMBOI
COUNSEL TO COMMISSIONERS
AARON D. MASLOW
LEGAL COUNSEL

MARIETTA A. LIGUORI
CHIEF CLERK
LEO A. BARRILE
DEPUTY CHIEF CLERK

BROOKLYN BOROUGH OFFICE

DATE_____

APPLICATION IS HEREBY MADE FOR VOTING INFORMATION THAT APPEARS ON THE REGISTRATION RECORDS IN THE COUNTY OF KINGS.

I UNDERSTAND THERE IS A FEE OF THREE ($ 3.00) DOLLARS PER PERSON FOR A COMPUTER SEARCH AND PRINTOUT ON ACTIVE VOTERS RECORDS OR A LETTER STATING THAT NO RECORD WAS FOUND. FOR THE OTHER FOUR BOROUGHS THE SAME SERVICE CAN BE PROVIDED FOR AN ADDITIONAL FEE OF $ 3.00 EACH.

FOR A TRANSCRIP OR PHOTO COPY OF NON ACTIVE VOTERS THE FEE IS $15.00. PRIOR TO 1957 NO RECORD CAN BE LOCATED WITHOUT THE VOTERS ADDRESS. (OLD RECORDS)

PAYMENT IS TO BE MADE TO THE BOARD OF ELECTION BY CERTIFIED CHECK OR MONEY ORDER. NO PERSONAL CHECKS WILL BE ACCEPTED . THE FEES ARE NON-REFUNDABLE.

NAME OF PERSON_____YEAR_____

LAST KNOWN ADDRESS_____

DATE OF BIRTH OR APPROXIMATE AGE: _____

APPLICANT NAME AND ADDRESS: _____

New York City Board of Elections Voter Registration Ledger Book

1. Registration no. _____
2. No. on enrolled blank _____
3. Party of enrolled voter _____
4. Residence no. _____
5. Name of street or avenue _____
6. No. umber of room or floor occupied by voter _____
7. Surname _____
8. Christian name _____
9. No. on public counter machine No.1 }General Election _____
10. No. on public counter machine No.2 } _____
11. No. on public counter machine No.1 }Special Election _____
12. No. on public counter machine No.2 } _____
13. No. on ballot delivered to voter }Fall primary _____
14. No. on ballot voted } _____
15. Age _____
16. Married, single, or widowed _____
17. In state (no. of years) _____
18. In county (no. of months) _____
19. In ED (no. of days) _____
20. Country of nativity _____
21. Date and court of naturalization; if citizen by marriage, name of person to whom married _____
22. Name of householder, tenant, of apt. lessee with whom reside _____
23. Last voted at: state
    city
    street address _____
24. Last voted in (year) _____
25. Business connection _____
26. Location of business _____
27. Signature on registration day _____
28. Signature on election day _____
29. Remarks _____

Repository _____; Film number _____; Volume and page _____; Date researched _____
Copy of original made _____?; Researcher's Notes: _____

Part IV

International and Other Records

International Tracing Service (ITS)

Forms Provided

    A.   *American Red Cross Tracing Inquiry, Form 1609*
    B.   *International Tracing Service: Index Card of Victim Information*
    C.   *International Tracing Service: Tracking Record*
    D.   *International Tracing Service: Index Record*
    E.   *International Tracing Service: Index Card of an Inquiry*

What is Available

The International Tracing Service (ITS), a component of the International Committee of the Red Cross (ICRC), maintains 40 million index cards mostly on survivors but also some on victims of the Holocaust. These cross reference information on the names appearing in any of the ITS archival documents. Most date from the 1940s. The principal purposes of the ITS are to assist in providing information on the fate of missing family members, to assist in providing certification of internment that could lead to the payment of reparations, and, in increasingly rare cases, to reunite families separated by war. Unfortunately, genealogical requests are considered low priority and it may take years for a reply to be received—if ever.

Where to Find Them

Originals of the records are located at ITS headquarters in Arolsen, Germany and can be accessed only via submission of Red Cross Form 1609 through the process outlined below. A duplicate set of about 16 million of those cards of particularly Jewish interest was filmed by Yad Vashem in Jerusalem and is available for in-person search or through an Israeli researcher. The abstract forms provided here are replicas of the four major types of cards in the Master Index and can be used to record information in in-person searches at Yad Vashem.

Detailed information on what is included in the record group, the cataloging system, and how to conduct searches, is contained in the Sack article, referenced below.

What You Need Before You Search

According to the Red Cross Fact Sheet (see below), the tracing process works as follows:
1. The inquirer phones the local Red Cross chapter to speak with a paid or volunteer caseworker.
2. The caseworker sends out Form 1609 which is completed and returned by the inquirer. (It is important that information such as names, dates, spellings, etc., on the form be verified carefully. Attachments can be added.)
3. After the form is returned, the caseworker opens a case file on the inquirer and forwards the forms to the Holocaust and War Victims Tracing and Information Center (HWVTIC), a unit of the American Red Cross in Baltimore. (4700 Mount Hope Drive, Baltimore, MD 21215-3231; phone: (800) 848-9277.
4. The Center workers in Baltimore enter the search information into its computerized database, and assign it a unique number.
5. Volunteers translate the inquiry into German and forward the translated form to ITS in Arolsen.
6. In addition to ITS, the Center's volunteers may contact the U.S. Social Security Administration, U.S. Immigration and Naturalization Service, and other Red Cross societies if there is reason to believe that such contact may lead to a successful search. Progress reports may be sent through the local chapter or directly by ITS to the inquirer.
7. When a response is received from ITS or another society, a letter is sent to the local chapter and forwarded to the inquirer.

Tips

- Some people have had responses from ITS, but genealogical requests evidently are given the lowest tracing priority. Be prepared for a frustratingly long wait for a reply. However, there are reports that the HWVTIC has arranged with ITS to provide a preliminary report within four months of an inquiry being filed. The Yad Vashem cards are far more accessible and can be searched in person.
- The four Master File cards are replicas of the cards in the ITS microfilm files located in Yad Vashem. They can be used for in-person search of the files as an alternative to photocopying.
- Cards are for survivors only, not for those who perished.
- Cards include those searching and those being searched for.

Additional Help

American Red Cross Holocaust and War Victims Tracing and Information Center, "Fact Sheet: Tracing Service for Holocaust and Other World War II Victims," (Arolsen, Germany, no date).

International Committee of the Red Cross, *International Tracing Service* (Arolsen, Germany: ITS, 1993).

International Committee of the Red Cross, Annual Report: International Tracing Service, <http://www.icrc.org>, May 1995.

International Tracing Service, *ITS: International Tracing Service,* Publication ITS 1993 - E 3000 (Arolsen, Germany: ITS, 1993).

Kurzweill, Arthur, *From Generation to Generation: How to Trace Your Jewish Genealogy and Family History* (NY: Schocken Books, revised 1994).

Mokotoff, Gary, *How to Document Victims and Locate Survivors of the Holocaust* (Teaneck, NJ: Avotaynu, Inc., 1995).

Sack, Sallyann Amdur, "International Tracing Service Records at Yad Vashem," *Avotaynu,* vol. X, No. 1, Spring 1994.

_____, and the Israel Genealogical Society. *A Guide to Jewish Genealogical Resources in Israel: Revised Edition* (Teaneck, New Jersey: Avotaynu, 1995).

TRACING INQUIRY

Instructions: Print or type. Prepare original plus three copies.
Forward original and two copies to:
   Foreign Location Inquiry Service
   American Red Cross
   18th & D Streets, N.W.
   Washington, DC 20006

Date _____

Person sought is my:

_____

A. INFORMATION ON PERSON SOUGHT

1. a. Complete Name _____ ☐ Male ☐ Female
   (Circle Family Name)

   b. Other Names Used _____ Maiden Name _____

2. Date of Birth or Approximate Age _____ Marital Status _____
   (Month, Day, Year)

3. Place of Birth _____
   (Town, City, or Province and Country)

4. Last Known Address (Include Street Number, Building, Town, State or Province, Country, Telephone Number, and Date of Address.)

   _____
   _____
   _____
   _____

5. Father's Full Name _____

6. Mother's Full Name _____ (Maiden Name) _____

7. Wife's or Husband's Name _____

8. Nationality _____ Ethnic Group _____

9. a. Occupation _____

   b. Address of Last Known Employer _____

10. Source and Date of Last News _____

11. Names and Addresses of Persons Who May Assist in Location

    _____
    _____
    _____

•OVER•

American Red Cross Form 1609 (Rev. 1-84)

Tips

- Some people have had responses from ITS, but genealogical requests evidently are given the lowest tracing priority. Be prepared for a frustratingly long wait for a reply. However, there are reports that the HWVTIC has arranged with ITS to provide a preliminary report within four months of an inquiry being filed. The Yad Vashem cards are far more accessible and can be searched in person.
- The four Master File cards are replicas of the cards in the ITS microfilm files located in Yad Vashem. They can be used for in-person search of the files as an alternative to photocopying.
- Cards are for survivors only, not for those who perished.
- Cards include those searching and those being searched for.

Additional Help

American Red Cross Holocaust and War Victims Tracing and Information Center, "Fact Sheet: Tracing Service for Holocaust and Other World War II Victims," (Arolsen, Germany, no date).

International Committee of the Red Cross, *International Tracing Service* (Arolsen, Germany: ITS, 1993).

International Committee of the Red Cross, Annual Report: International Tracing Service, <http://www.icrc.org>, May 1995.

International Tracing Service, *ITS: International Tracing Service,* Publication ITS 1993 - E 3000 (Arolsen, Germany: ITS, 1993).

Kurzweill, Arthur, *From Generation to Generation: How to Trace Your Jewish Genealogy and Family History* (NY: Schocken Books, revised 1994).

Mokotoff, Gary, *How to Document Victims and Locate Survivors of the Holocaust* (Teaneck, NJ: Avotaynu, Inc., 1995).

Sack, Sallyann Amdur, "International Tracing Service Records at Yad Vashem," *Avotaynu,* vol. X, No. 1, Spring 1994.

_____, and the Israel Genealogical Society. *A Guide to Jewish Genealogical Resources in Israel: Revised Edition* (Teaneck, New Jersey: Avotaynu, 1995).

TRACING INQUIRY

Instructions: Print or type. Prepare original plus three copies. Forward original and two copies to:
  Foreign Location Inquiry Service
  American Red Cross
  18th & D Streets, N.W.
  Washington, DC 20006

Date _____

Person sought is my:
_____

A. INFORMATION ON PERSON SOUGHT

1. a. Complete Name _____ ☐ Male ☐ Female
      (Circle Family Name)

   b. Other Names Used _____ Maiden Name _____

2. Date of Birth or Approximate Age _____ Marital Status _____
   (Month, Day, Year)

3. Place of Birth _____
   (Town, City, or Province and Country)

4. Last Known Address (Include Street Number, Building, Town, State or Province, Country, Telephone Number, and Date of Address.)

   _____
   _____
   _____
   _____

5. Father's Full Name _____

6. Mother's Full Name _____ (Maiden Name) _____

7. Wife's or Husband's Name _____

8. Nationality _____ Ethnic Group _____

9. a. Occupation _____

   b. Address of Last Known Employer _____

10. Source and Date of Last News _____

11. Names and Addresses of Persons Who May Assist in Location

    _____
    _____
    _____

•OVER•

American Red Cross Form 1609 (Rev. 1-84)

12. Additional Information See a, b, and c Below. _____

_____
_____
_____

Please provide as applicable:
a. Sought person's boat number, boat leader's name, and date and place of departure from home country.
b. For presumed prisoners of war or political detainee: military unit, rank, serial number, date of capture, and place of capture.
c. Foreign I.D. number, schools, health conditions, disabilities, and so on.

13. Accompanying Family Members (If Known)

FULL NAME	DOB (Day, Month, Year) OR APPROXIMATE AGE	SEX	RELATIONSHIP TO PERSON SOUGHT
1.			
2.			
3.			

B. INFORMATION ON INQUIRER

14. a. Complete Name _____ ☐ Male ☐ Female
       (Circle Family Name)

    b. Other Names Used _____

    c. Parents' Names _____
                        (Father)   (Mother)

15. Complete Address and Telephone Number_____
_____

16. Date of Birth _____ Place of Birth _____
                   (Month, Day, Year)

17. Nationality _____ Ethnic Group _____

_____
(If Naturalized, Please Provide Original Name if Different From Name Above.)

18. Reason(s) for Loss of Contact and Purpose of Search:

19. I Authorize the Release of My Address to the Person Sought.

_____   _____
         Signature of Inquirer   Date (Day, Month, Year)

C. CHAPTER NAME AND ADDRESS (To Be Completed by the Chapter)

_____   _____
         Name of Caseworker   Date

International Tracing Service Index Record: Index Card of Victim Information

Date
Name   File
BD   BP   Nat
Next of Kin
Source of Information
Last kn. Location   Date
CC/Prison   Arr.   lib.
Transf. on   to
Died on   in
Cause of death
Buried on   in
Grave   D.C.No.
Remarks

Repository _____ ; Film number _____ ; Volume and page_____ ; Date researched _____ ; Copy of original made _____ ?; Researcher's Notes:

International Tracing Service Index Record: Tracking Record

Name:

BD **BP** **Nat**

Repository _____; Film number _____; Volume and page_____; Date researched _____; Copy of original made _____?; Researcher's Notes:

A Selection of Reproducible Genealogy Forms and Tips for Using Them

International Tracing Service: Index Record

| Suchst.

Name Vornamen

Geb.-Tag geborene

Geb.-Orf Nation

Gestorben in

2	3	4	5	6	7	8	9	10

Bem.:

Repository _____ ;Filmnumber _____ ;Volume and page _____ ;Date researched _____ ;Copy of original made _____ ?; Researcher's Notes:

International Tracing Service: Index Card of an Inquiry

Name: T/D. No.:

Nee: Nat:

B.D.:   Rel:

B.P.:

Address:

Occupation

Last news:

Date:

Enquirer's name:

Address:

Relation:

Repository _____ ; Film number _____ ; Volume and page _____ ; Date researched _____ ; Copy of original made _____ ?; Researcher's Notes:

Hamburg Emigration Lists

Forms Provided

- A. *Historic Emigration Office search form*
- B. *Hamburg Passenger Record: Regular Index Record*
- C. *Hamburg Emigration Records recording form*

What Records are Available

Nearly one-third of the people who emigrated from central and eastern Europe between 1850 and 1934 sailed from the port of Hamburg, Germany. Fortunately, meticulous passenger lists were maintained and preserved. They are fully indexed. The lists provide such important genealogical information as age, occupation, birthplace or last residence, exact sailing date, ship's name, and destination. The lists are organized into two main categories: "direct," those who sailed directly to their destination (e.g., Hamburg to New York); and "indirect," those who had an intermediate destination (e.g., Liverpool or Antwerp). Indexes for each of these enable searches to be done. References below describe in detail how the indexes are used and include many helpful hints on using the indexes and the lists.

Where to Find Them

The records are available from two principal sources:
- Historic Emigration Office, P.O. Box 10 22 49, 20015 Hamburg, Germany. It will do a search of one name for one year for $60.
- The Family History Library has a complete duplicate microfilm set which can be searched at any of its Family History Centers or in Salt Lake City, catalogued under Germany, Hamburg, Hamburg-Emigration and Immigration.

What You Need Before You Search

Indexes generally are grouped in periods ranging from two months to about two years depending on the passenger volume, and are alphabetized only by the first letter of the surname. In addition to the name, therefore, the more precisely the sailing date is known, the fewer indexes will need to be searched.

Tips

- Before an in-person search is conducted at a FHC or other location, carefully read about and understand the anomalies of the indexing system. The LDS *Resource Guide* is a particularly useful source. It can save many wasted hours.
- If the person is found in the index, note all the information on the Index record form. The year and page number on the index are the key to finding the record on actual lists. (The Index Form shown is a sample. They vary over time, and apply only to the annual index. The 15-year index (1856–71) uses a different format.
- Column headings on the passenger lists may vary according to shipping line and year; the replica provided was used around 1899. Glossaries of column headings are included in the Shlyter article and the *Resource Guide* . . . published by the Family History Library.
- Although Hamburg was a major embarkation port, many Jewish immigrants sailed from other ports. It's worth the trouble, but not all searches will be successful.
- When families traveled together, typically only the husbands were indexed. Persons traveling together will usually appear on the same page of the lists.

- The most important piece of information provided is the name of the town in Europe the passenger originated from.

Additional Help

Colletta, John P., *They Came in Ships* (Salt Lake City: Ancestry, Inc., Revised 1993), pp. 45–46.

Ferguson, Laraine K. "Hamburg, Germany, Gateway to the Ancestral Home." *German Genealogical Digest,* vol. 2, no. 1 (1986), pages 10–14.

Resource Guide: The Hamburg Passenger Lists, 1850-1934. Research Paper Series C, No. 30. (Salt Lake City: The Genealogical Department, The Church of Jesus Christ of Latter Day Saints, no date).

Shlyter, Daniel M, "Hamburg Passenger Lists," in *The Encyclopedia of Jewish Genealogy, Volume I: Sources in the United States and Canada,* edited by Arthur Kurzweil and Miriam Weiner (Northvale, NJ: Jason Aronson, Inc,, 1991), pp. 9-12.

Siegel, Steven. "Researching the Hamburg Passenger Lists." *Dorot*, Winter 1992–93.

Sielemann, Jurgen, "Eastern European Jewish Emigration via the Port of Hamburg: 1880-1914," in *The Encyclopedia of Jewish Genealogy,* pp. 7-9.

_____, "Records Regarding Emigrants in the Hamburg State Archives," presentation at the International Seminar on Jewish Genealogy, Salt Lake City, UT, July 1991.

Tepper, Michael, *American Passenger Arrival Records: A Guide to the Records of Immigrants at American Ports by Sail and Steam* (Baltimore: Genealogical Publishing Company, Revised, 1993), pp. 129-132.

Hamburg Emigration Office Search Form

Written requests

Acknowledgement of receipt:

(to be filled out by the Historic Emigration Office)

Order No.:

(to be filled out by the Historic Emigration Office)

Sender

Please send your written request to the:

Hamburg Tourist Board

HISTORIC EMIGRATION OFFICE
P.O. Box 10 22 49 · 20015 Hamburg
Germany

✂ Please cut on dotted line

Determining your ancestors' exact emigration year

If you do not know the exact year your ancestors emigrated to the New World there are two ways to determine it.

In the USA
You should know what state your ancestors settled in for a longer period.
A population census was taken every 10 years in the USA. Immigrants were recorded in the U.S. Census Records. These records are on microfilm and can be looked into in any larger public library. Some of these records contain the exact year of immigration which is of utmost importance in finding your ancestors' records at the HEO.

In Germany
You should know the name of town your ancestors lived in until they emigrated to the USA.
In the 19th century, German citizens were required to apply for emigration with the German authorities. The State Archives contain records of birthplaces or hometowns as well as the application forms emigrants were required to fill out.

The Historic Emigration Office mailing address is:

Hamburg Tourist Board

HISTORIC EMIGRATION OFFICE
P.O. Box 10 22 49 · 20015 Hamburg
Germany

Hamburg Emigration Office Search Form

And this is how it works

Simply fill out the search form in capital letters and send to the HISTORIC EMIGRATION OFFICE in Hamburg or visit us personally.

Every detail helps us find your ancestors. If you have copies of any documents, such as passport, German discharge papers, birth or wedding certificates, copies from church records or U.S. Census Records, declaration of intention, ship passenger arrival list, please be sure to include them with your written request or bring them along.

Please include a check for US $ 60. The fee is the same whether or not our search is successful.

A search may take up to eight months to complete. Requests are processed in order of arrival.

Come visit us personally at the:

HISTORIC EMIGRATION OFFICE
c/o Tourist Information office in the Port of Hamburg
St. Pauli-Landungsbrücken between piers 4 and 5
Mon. – Sat. from 9 A.M. – 6 P.M.
Nov. – Feb. from 10 A.M. – 5 P.M.
Tel. (40) 300 51 - 250

For further information on Hamburg please contact:

Hamburg
North America Representation
38 West 32nd Street, Suite 1210
New York, N.Y. 10001
Tel. (212) 967-3110
Fax (212) 629-6052

Publisher: Hamburg Tourist Board
P.O. Box 10 2249, 20015 Hamburg
Photos: Ev. Auslandsberatung f. Auswanderer, Auslandstätige und Ausländer-Ehen eV / Thomas Hampel (cover), Thomas Grimm, Thomas Hampel, Urs F. Kluyver, Fritz Mader, Karl-Heinz Petersen, G. P. Reichelt, Staatliche Landesbildstelle / Johann und Heinrich Hamann, Studio Pierer

---

Written requests

Exact emigration year:

First and last names of emigrant

Age at time of emigration, if known

Hometown or region where ancestor lived, if known

Profession, if known

Name of ship, if known

Name and age of other family members who emigrated at same time

Other details

Hamburg Passenger Record: Regular Index Record

1. Name of ship _____

2. Ship departure date _____

3. Name of passenger _____

4. Ship captain's name _____

5. Ship's port of destination _____

6. Page on which the passenger record is found _____

Repository _____; Film number _____; Volume and page_____; Date researched _____; Copy of original made _____?; Researcher's Notes:

Hamburg Passenger Record

Column	Heading
1	*(Number on list)* _____
2	Zuname *(Surname)* _____
3	Vornamen *(Given names)* _____
4	Geschlecht--mannlich, weiblich *(Sex--male, female)* _____
5	Alter *(Age)* _____
6	Bei deutsch Mannern v. 17 bis 25 Jahren: Ist die Entlassungsurkunde oder das Zeugniss 23 des Ausweges vorgelegt? *(For German men between 17 and 25 years: Has the bill of release or testimony for article 23 concerning a release been presented?)* _____
7	Familiaenstand--ledig, u.s.w. *(Family status--single, etc.)* _____
8	Bisheriger Wohnort *(Previous residence)* _____
9	Staatsangehorigkeit *(Citizenship)* _____
10	Bezeichnung des bisherigen Berufa *(Indication of previous occupation)* _____
11	Stellung im Berufe *(Position in profession)* _____
12	Ziel der Auswanderung--Ort and Staat *(Destination, place and country should be given)* _____
13	Davon sind *(of those the following are)* • Erwachsene und Kinder uber 8 Jahr *(Adults and children over 8 years)* _____ • Kinder unter 8 Jaher *(Children under 8 years)* _____

Repository _____ ; Film number _____ ; Volume and page _____ ; Date researched _____ ; Copy of original made _____ ?; Researcher's Notes:

Polish Vital Records

Forms Provided

- A. *Birth Record*
- B. *Marriage Record*
- C. *Death Record*

What is Available

Nineteenth century vital records from numerous Polish communities have survived as a resource of incalculable genealogical value. Even though Poland did not exist as a sovereign state from 1795 to 1917, the records were maintained by local authorities in a fairly standardized (Napoleonic) format. Although the number of records that have survived from individual towns varies considerably, most tend to cover the period from around 1826 up to the present. Records older than 100 years are transferred to the Polish archive system; records more recent than 100 years old are maintained in the office of the issuing agency. Jewish records usually were separate from other civil records but may be intermingled in some communities, particularly in earlier years and smaller communities.

Similar records for countries of the former Soviet Union are slowly becoming available; many Belarussian and other records are being filmed by the FHL. Although lists of Polish communities for which the FHL has filmed these records have been compiled (see *Encyclopedia of Jewish Genealogy*, below), filming continues and these lists now are out of date. The best source is the most recent FHL catalog which usually is updated annually.

Finally, the Jewish Genealogy Discussion Group on the Internet has undertaken the task of compiling an index to selected Polish vital records that will be available for electronic searching. See the Russian Era Indexing of Poland Project (REIPP) InfoFile, below.

Where to Find Them

There are basically two sources of records. The FHL has a vast collection of Polish Jewish vital records accessible through its catalog. Most date from before 1880. These can be searched in person. They are cataloged under Poland [Province] [Town]—Jewish Records. Because most towns compiled annual indexes, individual records may be found even by researchers lacking knowledge of the Polish language (or Russian for some areas after 1866). The other means of obtaining such records is by directing an inquiry to the Polish State Archives which, in turn, will forward it to the appropriate regional archive for searching. The address for the Archives is: Naczelna Dyrekcja, Archiwów Państwowych, ul. Dluga 6, Skr. Poczt. Nr. 1005, 00-950 Warszawa, Poland. (See the "Vital Records in Poland" InfoFile for details.)

Either way, the results will be a photocopy of the original in the original language. The forms provided here will facilitate recording the information and having it translated.

What You Need Before You Search

As with any other vital records search, the information needed for an in-person search (at a FHC) is name of town, approximate year the event (birth, marriage, death) occurred, and a reasonably close spelling of the surname in the original Polish.

Tips

- The information provided here is only a brief introduction to a complex subject. Carefully review Frazin's or Shea's books. In addition to their value as translation guides, they explain in detail how the records are organized

- and formatted.
- Typically, a town's record book will start with birth records, followed by birth index, marriage records, marriage index, death records, death index. One efficient way to search is to unwind the reel all the way to the end, and work your way backwards, first checking each index and then its corresponding records.
- If searching for many records of a family that resided in a town for a long period of time, consider making photocopies of the entire set of indexes. For towns up to 10,000 people, a full set of annual indexes will probably be under 10 pages. A sixty-year set of records will therefore be a less-than 600 page reference of considerable value as each record found leads to additional generations or new families by marriage. These can be shared with researchers interested in the same town (through the REIPP).
- Although the record forms are fairly standardized, there are variations, as fully explained in Frazin and Shea's translation guides. The forms provided here—Polish above, the English translation below—are commonly used but no assurance is given they will be appropriate for all records.
- Be prepared for gaps in the records. Some towns did no indexes; some that usually provided index occasionally missed a year; and the books are old and many pages or whole volumes may be missing.
- Learn where the names are located within each record so that, if an index is missing, you can search the individual records fairly quickly. The Polish spellings are close to their English equivalents, but the signatures are usually in Yiddish.
- Very small shtetls did not have local civil authorities. Records were filed at offices in nearby larger towns, Gazetteers and good historic maps may be needed to determine where such records might be maintained.

Additional Help

Cymbler, Jeffrey, "Polish-Jewish Genealogical Research," *Avotaynu,* vol. IX, no. 2, Summer 1993.

Davis, Lauren B. Eisenberg, "Polish Vital Records for the Very Beginner: The Polish Language Challenged," *Avotaynu,* vol. XI, no. 4, Winter 1995.

"Directory of Polish State Archives," *Avotaynu,* vol. X, no. 1, Spring 1994.

Frazin, Judith R., *A Translation Guide to 19th Century Polish Language Civil-Registration Documents* (Northbrook, IL: Jewish Genealogical Society of Illinois, Second Edition, 1989).

JewishGen InfoFile, "Russian Era Indexing of Poland Project," <http://www.jewishgen.org>, March 1996.

JewishGen InfoFile, "Tracing Your Roots in Poland," <http://www.jewishgen.org>, Dec. 1995.

JewishGen InfoFile, "Vital Records in Poland," <http://www.jewishgen.org>, Dec. 1995.

"Polish-Jewish Records at the Family History Library, Salt Lake City, Utah," in *Encyclopedia of Jewish Genealogy,* pp. 202–215 (reprinted from *Avotaynu,* vol. II, no. 1, 1986.

Shea, Jonathan D., and William F. Hoffman, *Following the Paper Trail: A Multilingual Translation Guide.* (New Milford, CT: Language and Lineage Press, 1991).

Shea, Jonathan D., *Russian Language Documents from Russian Poland: A Translation Manual for Genealogists.* (Orem, UT: Genun Publishers, c/o Genealogy Unlimited, 1989).

Polish Birth Record (Post-1826)

Record Number_____; Index Number_____

(1)**Dzialo sie** (date, time, location)

(2)**stawil sie** (father)

(3)**w obecnosci swiadkow** (witnesses)

(4)**okazal nam** (sex, date, time)

(5)**z Malzonki Iego** (wife, age, maiden name)

(6)**Imie** (child's name)

(7)**Akt ten** (conclusion)

(8)**Signatures**

----

(1)**It happened [took place] in** (place)
on (date, time)

(2)**Came [presented himself]** (name)
(occupation)
(age)
(residence)

(3)**in the presence of witnesses** (witnesses names, occupations, ages)

(4)**he showed to us** (sex, where born, date, time)

(5)**from his wife** (name, age, etc.)

(6)**the name** (name)

(7)**This document** (read, signed, etc.)

(8)**Signatures of witnesses**

Repository _____ ; Film number _____ ; Volume and page _____ ; Date researched _____ ; Copy of original made _____ ?; Researcher's Notes:

Polish Marriage Record (Post-1826)

Record Number_____; Index Number_____

(1)**Dzialo sie [took place] in** (place, date, time)

(2)**wraz z + name + kawaralem** (groom, age)

(3)**z [born]** (parents names, facts)

(4)**I + name + panna** (and + name + unmarried girl)

(5)**z [born] from** (parents' names, facts)

(6)**w przytomnosci swiadkow** (in the presence of witnesses)

(7)**oswiadczyl** (marriage date)

(8)**miedzy** (between [bride and groom])

(9)**zapowiedzi** (dates, places of marriage banns and marriage ceremony)

(10)**akt ten** (read and signed, etc).

(11)**signatures of witnesses, groom, bride, etc.**

----

(1)**It happened [took place] in** (place, date, time)

(2)**together with** (groom, age)

(3)**[born] from** (parents names, facts)

(4)**and + name + unmarried girl** (bride)

(5)**[born] from** (parents' names, facts)

(6)**in the presence of witnesses** (names, facts)

(7)**stated** (marriage date)

(8)**between** (restatement of names of bride, groom)

(9)**the banns** (banns and marriage ceremony)

(10)**this document read, signed, etc.)**

(11)**signatures of witnesses, groom, bride, etc.**

Repository_____; Film number_____; Volume and page_____; Date researched_____; Copy of original made_____?; Researcher's Notes:

A Selection of Reproducible Genealogy Forms and Tips for Using Them • 121

Polish Death Record (Post-1826)

Record Number_____; Index Number_____

(1)**dzialo sie** (document date, time, location)

(2)**stawili sie** (witnesses and facts about them)

(3)**oswiadczyli** (they stated (death date, hour, location)

(4)**umarl(a)** (place of death & name of deceased + age, occupation, possibly date & place of birth & parents' names)

(5)**pozostawiwszy po sobie** ((names, relationships & possibly ages of surviving family members, and property, if any)

(6)**po przekonaniu sie naocznem o zejsciu** (After being convinced with one's own eyes about [the] death of + repetition of deceased's name, & statement that the document was read to the witnesses & signed)

(7)**Signatures** (official & witnesses, not usually surviving relatives)

---

(1)**It happened [took place]** (document date, time, location)

(2)**came [presented themselves]** (witnesses and facts about them)

(3)**they stated** (death date, hour, location)

(4)**died** (place of death & name of deceased + age, occupation, possibly date & place of birth & parents' names)

(5)**after the deceased they were left behind** (names, relationships & possibly ages of surviving family members, and property, if any)

(6)**After being convinced with one's own eyes about [the] death of + repetition of deceased's name, & statement that the document was read to the witnesses & signed)

(7)**Signatures** (official & witnesses, not usually surviving relatives)

Repository _____; Film number _____; Volume and page _____; Date researched _____; Copy of original made _____?; Researcher's Notes:

American Gathering of Jewish Holocaust Survivors

Forms Provided

    A.   *National Registry of Jewish Holocaust Survivors: Family Registry*
    B.   *American Gathering of Jewish Holocaust Survivors: Family Registry: Search Form*

What Records are Available

The American Gathering maintains a growing list now numbering more than 65,000 Holocaust survivors and family members. For about 20,000 of these survivors, they have additional information such as place of birth and where they were during the Holocaust.

Where to Find Them

All the records are located at the offices of the American Gathering, 122 West 30th Street, Suite 205, New York, NY 10001. However, the organization has published all of its names on file, fully cross-indexed. This listing is likely to be available in Holocaust centers and Jewish libraries. A successor list, the Registry of Jewish Holocaust Survivors, is located at the U.S. Holocaust Memorial Museum in Washington, DC, but is currently accessible only in person. General information is available at the USHMM's WWW homepage at <http://www.ushmm.org>.

What You Need Before You Search

See the form.

Tips

- Although the American Gathering will not supply addresses, it will forward letters. For example, letters can be sent to survivors from ancestral towns to learn about the town and possible links with former residents or Holocaust victims.

Additional Help

American Gathering of Jewish Holocaust Survivors, *National Registry of Jewish Holocaust Survivors* (New York: American Gathering, var. dates).

Mokotoff, Gary, *How to Document Victims and Locate Survivors of the Holocaust* (Teaneck, NJ: Avotaynu, Inc., 1995).

Please complete, if you have not yet done so, and return to:
AMERICAN GATHERING OF JEWISH HOLOCAUST SURVIVORS, 122 WEST 30TH STREET, SUITE 205, NEW YORK, NY 10001

National Registry of Jewish Holocaust Survivors

FAMILY REGISTRY #

NAME: _____

ADDRESS: _____

PHONE: _____ OCCUPATION: _____

Are you a survivor? yes/no
Are you 2nd generation? yes/no

Is your spouse a survivor? yes/no
Is your spouse a 2nd generation yes/no

Have you ever given an oral history (Yes/No) _____ if Yes, please give year and location? _____

If you are a survivor, complete the following:

Name before or during war or maiden name: _____

Place of birth: City _____ Country _____

Place of residence before war: City _____ Country _____

Places during war (list all): _____
Names of ghetto, concentration camps, partisan or hiding place.

_____

Spouse's name: _____ Occupation: _____

If your spouse is a Survivor, complete or correct the following:

Name before or during war or maiden name: _____

Place of birth: City _____ Country _____

Place of residence before war: City _____ Country _____

Places during war (list all): _____
Names of ghetto, concentration camps, partisan or hiding place.

_____

Other living members of your family (Survivors, 2nd Generation).
If members of your family are not shown please add them to the enclosed form so they may be included in the registry.

Name _____ Tel. _____
Address _____ Zip _____
This person is my: ☐ Mother ☐ Father ☐ Son ☐ Daughter ☐ Brother ☐ Sister

Name _____ Tel. _____
Address _____ Zip _____
This person is my: ☐ Mother ☐ Father ☐ Son ☐ Daughter ☐ Brother ☐ Sister

Name _____ Tel. _____
Address _____ Zip _____
This person is my: ☐ Mother ☐ Father ☐ Son ☐ Daughter ☐ Brother ☐ Sister

Name _____ Tel. _____
Address _____ Zip _____
This person is my: ☐ Mother ☐ Father ☐ Son ☐ Daughter ☐ Brother ☐ Sister

PHOTOGRAPHS

Please write the name(s) of the person, approximate date, and place where photo was taken in the appropriate box. Do not affix the picture to the page, we will do this in our office.

Picture Before WWII

NAME _____

DATE _____

PLACE _____

Picture After Liberation

NAME _____

DATE _____

PLACE _____

Recent Picture

NAME _____

DATE _____

PLACE _____

RECORD OF DECEASED FAMILY MEMBERS WHO CAME TO THE UNITED STATES AFTER THE HOLOCAUST

Relationship_____

Name_____

Residence before WWII _____
_____

Place during Holocaust _____
_____

Date and place of death _____

Age at time of death _____

Relationship_____

Name_____

Residence before WWII _____
_____

Place during Holocaust _____
_____

Date and place of death _____

Age at time of death _____

American Gathering of Jewish Holocaust Survivors

אמעריקאנער צוזאמענקום פון דער שארית הפליטה

122 West 30th Street • Suite 205 • New York, N.Y. 10001 • (212) 239-4230

NATIONAL REGISTER OF JEWISH HOLOCAUST SURVIVORS
SEARCH FORM

Instructions: Fill in as much information as you can.

1. *NAME OF THE PERSON YOU ARE SEEKING:* TYPE OR PRINT CLEARLY

   A. European Name: _____
                               Last Name   First Name

   B. American Name: _____
                               Last Name   First Name

2. *LOCATION:*

   A. Home town(s) before World War II (or place of birth):

Country	Region/Province	Town/City
Country	Region/Province	Town/City

   B. Place(s) of survival (e.g., camp, ghetto, hideout, forest):

   _____ Years: _____
   _____ Years: _____

   C. Current Residence (if known):

City	State/Province	Country

****

Your Registration No.: _____ Today's Date: _____

Your Name: _____

_____ Survivor   _____ Second Generation   _____ Spouse

Your Home Address: _____

_____ STATE _____ ZIP _____

RELEASE

I, _____, a registered participant in the
               (print your full name)

American Gathering of Jewish Holocaust Survivors, understand that the information I am requesting is confidential and is to be used solely to facilitate my reunion with other Jewish holocaust survivors and their families listed in the National Register. I agree that I will not use the information received in response to this request for any other purpose.

_____
Signature

The Church of Jesus Christ of Latter-day Saints: Request for Photocopies

Forms Provided

    A.   *Request for Photocopies*

What Records are Available

This form is used to request copies of any documents in the vast holdings of the Family History Library. If the Library has the record, and the specific record or page number is known, this form can provide a far less expensive way of getting copies than writing to the source. In other words, by using this form, virtually all the holdings of the FHL are made available by mail.

Where to Find Them

    By mail, to the address shown on the form.

What You Need Before You Search

    See the form.

Tips

- The Library does not do searches. The form is used only when a specific record or page number is known. That means that it may take several steps before the actual record can be obtained. If a search may require searching through many pages of an index, it is probably better to rent the microfilm through a Family History Center and then use the form to get the record.
- Since the FHL does not lend books—and it has many in its collection—this is a good way to get copies of individual pages.
- Follow the instructions. Staff of local FHCs are probably familiar with the form and can help researchers complete it properly.

THE CHURCH OF JESUS CHRIST OF LATTER-DAY SAINTS

Request for Photocopies—Census Records, Books, Microfilm or Microfiche

Mail your order to:
Family History Department
35 North West Temple Street
Salt Lake City, Utah 84150

For Patron Use Used to return your order	**For Family History Department Use**
Name and address (include country if *not* U.S.)	Family History Department mail services stamp
Telephone number ( )	Amount received in Family History Department $

For Family History Center Use *Do not collect money. The patron should mail this request with a check or money order.*

Family history center name	Family history center number

Instructions

1. Use this form to order photocopies of census records, books, microfilm or microfiche. *Please use a separate form for each type of request.* For example, do not use the same form to request copies from both a census record and book.
2. You may request copies from the index of a record. After you receive the index, you may send a second form requesting the specific pages you need.
3. Please provide all information necessary to identify the item to be copied.
4. The library may need to limit the number of copies or decline some photocopy requests because of copyright or other restrictions.
5. If you have any questions, please ask a staff member at the family history center to review your completed form before you mail it.
6. Please send your check or money order (payable to the Family History Department) with the forms. There is a $2.00 minimum.
   - $.25 (cents) for each copy when you provide page numbers.
   - $2.00 for each copy without a specific page number.

NOTICE WARNING CONCERNING COPYRIGHT RESTRICTIONS

The copyright law of the United States (Title 17, United States Code) governs the making of photocopies or other reproductions of copyrighted material.
Under certain conditions specified in the law, libraries and archives are authorized to furnish a photocopy or other reproduction. One of these specific conditions is that the photocopy or reproduction is not to be "used for any purpose other than private study, scholarship, or research." If a user makes a request for, or later uses, a photocopy or reproduction for purposes in excess of "fair use," that user may be liable for copyright infringement.
This institution reserves the right to refuse to accept a copying order if, in its judgment, fulfillment of the order would involve violation of copyright law.

Census Records On Microfilm
Enumeration districts for British Census records are listed at the beginning of each district on the film.

Family History Library film number	Year	State/Province	County	Town/Parish/Village	Enum. district	Line	Sheet or page	Name of individual
EXAMPLE: 1,240,503	1900	Kansas	Wilson	Neodesha	171	7	14	Mikesell, David

General Microfilm/Microfiche
For copies from an International Genealogical Index source, use the form PFGS3264 (*Request for Photocopies—Inter. Gen. Index*).

Family History Library microfilm/microfiche number	Name of individual	Title or parents/spouse (if applicable)	Event date (if applicable)	Event place (if applicable)	Page or grid number
EXAMPLE: 101,161	John Brennan	Ireland Civil Registration of Births Thomas Brennan/Mary	24 Jan 1868	Cork, Cork, Ireland	581

U.S. Census Indexes on Microfiche (known as AIS)

AIS search number (from top right-hand side of fiche)	Microfiche no. (directly below AIS number)	Search locality and time period (from top center of fiche)	Grid numbers	Surname
EXAMPLE: AIS 7	11	Midwestern and Western States 1850–1906	C12, D12, E12, F12, G12	Balch

Books

Family History Library book number	Title	Author	Individual or Family name	Page numbers
EXAMPLE: 994 H23w	Women in Australia	Daniels, Kay	Smith	pg. 6 and Index

Yad Vashem Pages of Testimony

Forms Provided

A. *Page of Testimony*

What Records are Available

The Yad Vashem Hall of Names has on file about 3 million pages of testimony for Holocaust victims, usually submitted by a relative. Most date from the 1950s. In addition to information about the individual and his or her family, the page includes the name and address of the person providing the testimony, a possible lead to surviving friends or relatives (see Search Bureau for Missing Relatives, below). The original pages are on paper, but all now are on microfiche. Recent efforts to computerize the pages have made much progress leading to much faster searches and less reliance on precise spellings of names. It also enables searches of relatively common names to be narrowed to specified communities.

The Page provided here is in English and Hebrew. Yad Vashem can provide copies in many languages.

Where to Find Them

All the Pages are on file at the Hall of Names at Yad Vashem, Har Hazikaron (Mount of Remembrance), P.O. Box 3477, Jerusalem 91034, Israel. Phone: 02-751-611. Fax: 02-433-511. WWW: <http://yvs.shani.net>.

What You Need Before You Search

A search can be requested—no form is needed—by providing surname, first name, and place of birth or residence. Of course, the more that is provided, the greater the likelihood of a successful search. The more common the name, the more information that must be included. For an uncommon name a "global" surname search can be performed. Search charges are inexpensive, with overall costs determined by the number of names provided. They will bill afterward. A search can also be submitted by electronic mail. See the JewishGen InfoFile, below.

Additional Help

JewishGen InfoFile, "Yad Vashem Hall of Names," <http://www.jewishgen.org>, July 1995.

JewishGen InfoFile, "Yad Vashem Hall of Names: Email Search," <http://www.jewishgen.org>, March 1996.

Mokotoff, Gary, *How to Document Victims and Locate Survivors of the Holocaust* (Teaneck, NJ: Avotaynu, Inc., 1995).

Sack, Sallyann Amdur, "More Resources in Israel," *Avotaynu,* vol. VIII, no. 2, Summer 1991.

Sack, Sallyann Amdur and the Israel Genealogical Society. *A Guide to Jewish Genealogical Resources in Israel: Revised Edition* (Teaneck, New Jersey: Avotaynu, 1995).

YAD VASHEM
יד ושם

The Holocaust Martyrs' and Heroes' Remembrance Authority   רשות הזיכרון לשואה ולגבורה

PAGES OF TESTIMONY

The Pages of Testimony (symbolic tombstones) are intended to serve as a lasting memorial for the victims of the Holocaust. The details beyond names and places provide a "personality" for an identity which would otherwise be lost in the coming generations. Accordingly, we require that:

1. Each victim of the Holocaust should be inscribed on a separate form. Please enter all information in BLOCK LETTERS. Ambiguous pages cannot be properly filed, and thus cannot be easily found.

2. A Page of Testimony is acceptable only if the family (or maiden) name is included. While many biographical details of the victim may not be known, the family name, and the first name and last place of residence, should be submitted. Unknown spouses and children may be registered as (wife of /son of/daughter of etc.,). All details which are known or partially known should be detailed, e.g., about 50 years, @ 1895, infant/baby are all better than a blank space.

3. Use Only Pages of Testimony that conform in size, text, colour and quality with the original Pages of Testimony issued by Yad Vashem.

4. Please SIGN and date the Pages of Testimony in the spaces specifically allotted.

5. Please specify that the victim perished during the Holocaust, even if further details are not available.(e.g. Holocaust - details unknown / or not heard from after 1939)

6. The Pages of Testimony are intended only for victims who perished during the Holocaust not later than October 1945. Do not register those who survived the Holocaust.

7. Enclosed you will find new forms to fill in and return to us at your earliest convenience.
PLEASE DO NOT FOLD

Sincerely,
Dept. Pages of Testimony

FOR YOUR INFORMATION:
To date, some 2 million pages have been recorded. Blank forms are available in 8 languages. In less than a generation there may be no-one living who personally remembers the victims. Interview your oldest living relatives for details on the victims before it is too late. (There is no fee required for registration, however, any contribution will be gratefully acknowledged.)

YAD VASHEM

**Martyrs' and Heroes'
Remembrance Authority
P.O.B. 3477 Jerusalem, Israel**

דף-עד

רשות-הזיכרון
לשואה ולגבורה, ירושלים

יד ושם

ירושלים, הר הזיכרון

ת.ד. 3477

THE MARTYRS' AND HEROES'
REMEMBRANCE LAW, 5713–1953
determines in article No. 2 that –

The task of YAD VASHEM is to gather into the homeland material regarding all those members of the Jewish people who laid down their lives, who fought and rebelled against the Nazi enemy and his collaborators, and to perpetuate their NAMES and those of the communities, organisations, and institutions which were destroyed because they were Jewish.

חוק זכרון השואה והגבורה - תשי"ג 1953
קובע בסעיף מס' 2:

תפקידו של יד-ושם הוא לאסוף אל המולדת את זכרם של כל אלה מבני העם היהודי, שנפלו ומסרו את נפשם, נלחמו ומרדו באויב הנאצי ובעוזריו, ולהציב **שם וזכר להם**, לקהילות, לארגונים ולמוסדות שנחרבו בגלל השתייכותם לעם היהודי.

(ספר החוקים מס' 132,
י"ז אלול תשי"ג (28.8.53

פרטי הניספה: נא לרשום את שמו של כל ניספה על דף נפרד ולכתוב באותיות דפוס ובנקוד
DETAILS OF VICTIM: INSCRIBE EACH VICTIM ON A SEPARATE PAGE, IN BLOCK LETTERS

1.	Family name:	שם משפחה מנוקד:	
2.	First name:	שם פרטי:	
3.	Previous name: (nee for woman)	שם משפחה קודם: (אישה, לפני נישואים)	
4.	Birth date or appr. age	תאריך לידה/גיל משוער:	
5.	Sex	מין	
6.	Fam. status	מצב משפחתי	
7.	Birth place and country:	מקום לידה וארץ:	

תמונת הניספה (דרכון)
נא לרשום את שמו של הניספה על הצד השני של התמונה

Victim's photo
write victim's name
on back side please

8.	Victim's mother	- First name: - Maiden name/nee:	- שם פרטי: - שם מהבית: אם הניספה
9.	Victim's father	- First name:	- שם פרטי: אב הניספה
10.	Victim's spouse	- First name: - Maiden name/nee:	- שם פרטי: - שם מהבית: בן-זוגו של הניספה
11.	Permanent residence place and country:		מקום מגורים קבוע וארץ:
12.	Wartime residence place and country:		מקום מגורים בזמן המלחמה וארץ:
13.	Date/year of death:	14. Victim's profession:	מקצוע הניספה: / תאריך/שנת המוות:
15.	Death place: Circumstances of death:		מקום המוות: ונסיבות המוות:

Reported by:

I, the undersigned _____

Residing at (address) _____

Relationship to victim (family/other) _____

פרטי המצהיר:

אני, החי"ם (שם) _____

הגר בכתובת _____

קירבה לניספה (משפחתית/אחרת) _____

מצהיר/ה בזה כי העדות שמסרתי על פרטיה היא נכונה ואמיתית לפי מיטב ידיעתי והכרתי
HEREBY DECLARE THAT THIS TESTIMONY IS CORRECT TO THE BEST OF MY KNOWLEDGE

Place and date _____ Signature _____ מקום ותאריך רישום / חתימה

"...ונתתי להם בביתי ובחומותי יד ושם..אשר לא יכרת". ישעיהו נו ה

"...even unto them will I give in mine house and within my walls a place and a name...that shall not be cut off." isaiah, lvi,5

Hebrew Immigrant Aid Society (HIAS) Location Service

Forms Provided

   A.   *HIAS Location Service*

What Records are Available

HIAS aided many Jewish immigrants starting from about 1900 until the present. It kept case files that are an excellent source of immigration information. Files may contain letters, immigration and naturalization information, records of efforts to unite families, etc. There are a variety of indexes to the various record groups that may include case number, dates and places of birth, names and relationship of families traveling together, last place of residence, destination, and information about arrival.

Where to Find Them

Searches can be done only by mailing the form to HIAS.

What You Need Before You Search

See the form.

Tips

- In addition to its own files, a HIAS search may extend to other sources, depending on the importance of the search.
- Pre-1937 files no longer exist; only the indexes remain.
- The Joint Distribution Committee (JDC) merged with HIAS in 1954; HIAS has access to indexes for these files.
- HIAS is in the process of computerizing its indexes. Currently, only post-1980 indexes have been done.
- Microfilm copies of the Arrival Index Cards, 1909-79, and other indexes can be viewed at the YIVO Institute for Jewish Research, 555 W. 57th Street, 11th Floor, New York, NY 10019 (212) 535-6700; fax (212) 734-1062.

Additional Help

Guzik, *Genealogical Resources in the New York Metropolitan Area*, pp. 39-40.

Date: _____

HIAS
333 Seventh Avenue
New York, NY 10001

LOCATION SERVICE SEARCH FORM

PERSON SOUGHT:

Name: _____
     (Last name)   (first name)   (maiden name)

Other names used _____ Occupation _____

Date of birth _____ City & country of birth _____

City & country of emigration _____

Date of arrival to country of emigration _____

Date of last communication _____

Father's name _____ Mother's name _____
                                                  (maiden name)

Other accompanying   Relationship   Birthdate/city &
family members   to person sought   country of birth

_____
_____
_____

* * * * * * * * * * * *

INQUIRER:

Name _____
     (last name)   (first name)   (maiden name)

Other names used _____ Arrival Date _____

Address _____

Telephone Number(s) _____

Date of birth _____ City & country of birth _____

Father's name _____ Mother's name _____
                                                  (maiden name)
Relationship to person sought _____

Other relevant information _____
_____
_____
_____

Doc. #0028d

HIAS LOCATION SERVICE FACT SHEET

HOW CAN WE ASSIST YOU?

If you are looking for someone with whom you have lost contact (or wish to establish contact), HIAS can conduct a search in the U.S. and abroad. We will need some basic information about the person you are seeking, such as first and last name, birthdate and birthplace, country of emigration, and when the last contact occurred.

Please note that we cannot guarantee that all searches will be successful. Searches may take from several months to more than a year.

HOW DO YOU REQUEST OUR LOCATION SERVICES?

1. Fill out the Location Form (enclosed) in English as completely as possible. <u>Please do not send photographs.</u>!

2. Mail the Location Form along with a $25 check or money order payable to HIAS. Make sure your last name appears on the check or money order.
   Mail to: **HIAS Location Service**
   333 Seventh Avenue
   New York, NY 10001

3. Within one month of your mailing, we will send you an acknowledgement receipt which will include your case number. Please refer to that number on any future inquiries.

HOW DO WE LOCATE PEOPLE?

We use appropriate sources of information, depending on the case. We work in cooperation with many organizations, including our U.S. affiliates and HIAS offices abroad, Jewish agencies worldwide and the International Tracing Service.

Once we have located the person sought, we request permission to release his/her address to the inquirer. If the person sought is interested in being contacted, we convey this information to the inquirer. Likewise we do not reveal the whereabouts of the person sought if he/she does not wish to be contacted.

HOW CAN YOU REACH US ONCE YOU HAVE APPLIED FOR OUR SERVICES (to provide or request further information on your case)?

Please call 212-613-1424. You may leave a message if an answering machine responds. Or you may write to us at the above address. Our hours are from 9:00 a.m. to 5:00 p.m. Monday through Friday.

Jewish Agency: Search Bureau for Missing Relatives

Forms Provided

A. *Search Request Form*

What Records are Available

The Search Bureau finds people who live—or ever have lived—in Israel. It has a card file, now computerized, and other resources, that lists names, addresses, and certain vital information on Israeli residents, as well as those who have inquired about them. It also has a computer file of every Israeli citizen who has died within the previous five years. Founded shortly after founding of the State, its original purpose was to aid in linking families separated by World War II. It has been used in every wave of migration since, most recently by Jews from the former Soviet Union. And it has been of enormous benefit to genealogists.

Where to Find Them

Write: Batya Unterschatz, Director, Search Bureau for Missing Relatives, P.O. Box 92, Jerusalem 91000 Israel. In person: 3 Ibn Givirol Street, Jerusalem. Phone: 972-2-612-471; fax: 972-2-202-516.

What You Need Before You Search

See the Inquiry Form.

Tips

- The form is useful, but not essential, for requesting a search. The Bureau, and its Director, Batya Unterschatz, is legendary for its ability to find missing people often with the most fragmentary information. In addition to its own extensive sources, the Bureau has access to a wide range of government records, including census records of the Department of the Interior. It is virtually the only source one should use if searching for someone in Israel.
- The Search Bureau has an on-line computer hookup with the Ministry of the Interior so it can locate official records. Although citizens are required to notify the Ministry of address changes, this is not always done promptly, so some addresses may be outdated. Similarly, names of people who died are not always dropped after five years, so some names may be retained on file for linger.
- A response might include some or all of the following, depending on what is available: surname, first name, parents' names, age, country of birth, date of arrival, spouse, children, name of ship on which an immigrant arrived, and recent name changes.
- The records may show if a person emigrated from Israel, possibly including where they went.
- In addition to searching for missing relatives, the Search Bureau can be used to locate:
  - Individuals who submitted Pages of Testimony memorializing victims of the Holocaust.
  - Editors of Yizkor books for towns of interest.
  - Heads of landsmanshaftn (the Search Bureau has a list of current societies).
  - The names and addresses of everyone from a given location that has been the subject of an inquiry.

Additional Help

Mokotoff, Gary, *How to Document Victims and Locate Survivors of the Holocaust* (Teaneck, NJ: Avotaynu, Inc., 1995).
Sack, Sallyann Amdur and the Israel Genealogical Society. *A Guide to Jewish Genealogical Resources in Israel: Revised Edition* (Teaneck, New Jersey: Avotaynu, 1995).